THE HUNTER'S DEVOTIONAL

STEVE CHAPMAN

HARVEST HOUSE PUBLISHERS
EUGENE, OREGON

Cover by Harvest House Publishers Inc.

Cover Illustrations © PaulPaladin, Askold Romanov / iStock.

THE HUNTER'S DEVOTIONAL
Copyright © 2016 Steve Chapman
Published by Harvest House Publishers
Eugene, Oregon 97408
www.harvesthousepublishers.com

Library of Congress Cataloging-in-Publication Data
Names: Chapman, Steve, author.
Title: The hunter's devotional / Steve Chapman.
Description: Eugene, Oregon : Harvest House Publishers, 2016.
Identifiers: LCCN 2015044105 (print) | LCCN 2016009752 (ebook) | ISBN 9780736967051 (hardcover) | ISBN 9780736967068 (eBook)
Subjects: LCSH: Hunting—Religious aspects—Christianity—Prayers and devotions.
Classification: LCC BV4597.4 .C424 2016 (print) | LCC BV4597.4 (ebook) | DDC 242/.68—dc23
LC record available at http://lccn.loc.gov/2015044105

Printed in China

19 20 21 22 23 24 / RDS-CD / 10 9 8 7 6 5 4

*To my two fellow hunters,
Lindsey Williams and Don Hicks,
who have often joined me in the woods and
faithfully prayed for me as I've traveled to speak
at game dinner events, and whose spiritual and
moral integrity inspire me to press on
to higher ground.*

Acknowledgment

My sincere thanks to my wife, Annie, for smiling supportively when I say as I head out to hunt, "Hey, Babe, I'm going to go do some book research!" I'm confident her prayers that God will use His great outdoors to speak to my heart have yielded many of the thoughts contained in these pages.

Contents

First Glimpse

There's hardly anything more exciting for a hunter than that first glimpse of the game that's being pursued. After putting a lot of effort (and expense) into preparing for the hunt, sometimes walking for miles or at other times sitting quietly for hours, to suddenly catch sight of the movement of an elusive animal or bird is a thrill that cannot be fully explained. One thing is for sure—each time it happens is one more good reason to go back and do it again.

In a similar way, when a person is on the hunt for a life-changing truth that is hidden in God's written Word and it suddenly comes into view, there is a rejoicing that erupts in the soul that is difficult to describe.

My hope is that this book will be carried by hunters to the deer woods, turkey fields, elk mountains, pronghorn prairies, water's-edge duck blinds, and any other place they go to engage in the exhilarating challenge of the fair chase. While they're waiting for the thrill of seeing the game, they can take a moment, read a page, and hopefully catch sight of a trophy of truth.

If this happens, the time I've invested in connecting the hunt for animals to the hunt for biblical insight will have been worth it. May God get the glory for He alone is the provider for meat that feeds both the body and the soul.

Steve Chapman

1

Hunting Expos

I am stirring up your sincere mind.

2 PETER 3:1

If you're a fan of outdoor shows and expos like I am, then I know that you, too, enjoy walking the aisles lined with booths featuring products that feed your passion for hunting. If I had all the cash I've laid out for tickets to these events I'd probably have enough for those two hundred acres of game-filled woods and fields I wish I had.

Have you ever noticed what time of the year these shows typically happen? It's usually around late summer that our events take place here in Middle Tennessee. If this time frame is the same for your area, did you ever wonder why they chose late summer for hunting shows? I have a theory.

The event planners took a poll among bona fide hunters to find out when they feel most frustrated they can't hunt. The results showed the longing to legally go chase something in the animal kingdom begins to build after turkey season closes in late spring and peaks around late July and August. It's when a serious hunter's trigger finger is twitching wildly, and he's about to burst with "want to."

I'm convinced the expo staff is sure that all they have to do to sell a ton of tickets is turn the heat up under the hunters' adrenalin pot that is already at a near boil. They do it by strategically putting up a picture of a big buck on a roadside billboard with a date, place, and show time. Once that's done, they know hunters will come running to the door. Why do I believe this works? Because it works on me.

Hunting show folks aren't the only ones who know the value of stirring up emotions that are already cooking. In the apostle Peter's second letter, he begins the third chapter with, "This is now, beloved, the second letter I am writing to you in which I am stirring up your sincere mind by way of reminder, that you should remember the words spoken beforehand by the holy prophets and the commandment of the Lord and Savior spoken by your apostles" (verses 1-2).

Peter was writing to Christians who were scattered throughout the world and were thought to be mostly Gentiles and not Jews. They were suffering because they were living in places where paganism and hostility led to many severe trials of their faith. Yet he knew in those who believed there was a hunger for peace, a longing for the persecution they were facing in the form of slander and violence to stop.

As a way of fostering or stirring up their hope, he urged them to not forget the words of the prophets as well as the commandments of Jesus that had been delivered to them by their apostles. His goal was to spur the Christians to hold fast to their faith in the face of their trials, to be "looking for and hastening the coming of the day of God," to be "looking for new heavens and a new earth, in which righteousness dwells," and to "be found by Him in peace, spotless and blameless" (verses 12, 13, and 14).

Peter's letter was a stirring one indeed, because it still stirs hearts to this day. I, for one, am deeply encouraged by it. I hope you'll take the time to read both of Peter's letters, because if you are looking forward to Christ's return, you'll be stirred by them even more than the news of a hunting expo that's coming.

Lord, You know how to get the spiritual juices flowing in me. You do it through the writers of Your recorded Word, and I thank You for it. Help me to understand and to never forget the precepts for right living that are found in the Bible. You are a kind Father for loving me enough to stir my heart, and Your timing is always perfect when it happens. Blessed be Your holy and exciting name! Amen.

2

Music in the High Grass

I called you but you did not answer.

JEREMIAH 7:13

Jason, Lindsey, and I arrived a little later than we wanted at the property we went to for a morning turkey hunt. We had to hurry to get our gear together, but within five minutes we were walking at a brisk pace to the far back field where we planned to set up. About three-quarters of the way there, I realized I had not silenced my phone like I normally do when I hunt.

Not wanting to slow us down, I wanted to turn the thing off while we were walking, so I felt for it in my belt holster, but it wasn't there. I whispered loud enough to be heard by my buddies, "Stop, guys! I've lost my phone."

I don't remember which one said it, but I got

some sympathy when I heard, "Oh, no! What a bummer!"

I stood still for a moment and mentally replayed our walk from our vehicles. My heart sank deeper when I remembered a lot of it was through some knee-high grass. I knew what I had to do.

"Guys, I hate to do it, but I gotta backtrack and see if I can find my phone. There's way too much information in it to not try to find it."

Then it hit me. I had not yet set it to silent.

"Lindsey, do you have your phone with you?"

I was relieved when he said, "I do."

"Can I use it to call my number? Maybe I'll hear my tone in the grass."

With Lindsey's phone in hand I retraced our path and called my number about every ten to fifteen yards. After nearly twenty calls I finally heard the faint sound of mandolin music in the distance. My custom call alert was definitely music to my ears.

When I rescued my phone I realized I would have never found it in the deep, thick grass where it had fallen without the other phone. I said a quick thanks to the Lord for helping me find it and headed to the field where Jason and Lindsey waited. I managed to rescue my wayward device and get back to my buddies a few minutes before the birds woke up. All was well.

When I got home that afternoon, I told Annie about using Lindsey's phone to find my phone and how sweet it was to hear it respond. She said, "I'm so happy for you," and then added a sobering truth. "If your phone had been off, you would have cried out, but your little lost lamb would not have heard and answered."

A little while later, Annie came into my man cave and said, "Forgive the pun, but your phone story has a familiar ring to it. If you'll look at Jeremiah 7, you'll see what I'm referring to."

I turned to my desktop and entered a web search for the verse. Sure enough, she was right. Speaking on behalf of God to the people of Israel, the prophet said, "'Because you have done all these things [broken several commandments and committed abominations],' declares the LORD, 'and I spoke to you, rising up early and speaking, but you did not hear, and I called you but you did not answer'" (verse 13).

Because the people chose not to answer God when He spoke to them about their sin, He warned them that He would cast them out of His sight. If they had been like my phone in the high grass that answered when I called it, they would not have faced such a horrible consequence.

I certainly wouldn't want to be silent if God called out to me. Instead, I want to do what Zacchaeus did when he heard Jesus say, "'Hurry and come down, for today I must stay at your house.' And he hurried and came down and received Him gladly" (Luke 19:5-6). Zacchaeus heard and answered. What Jesus said to him after he hit the ground told him that his life would never be the same. The Lord told him, "Today salvation has come to this house...For the Son of Man has come to seek and to save that which was lost" (verses 9-10).

That good news is as current today as it was then. If you haven't yet heard His call in your heart, whatever you do, when you hear it, make sure you answer so you, too, will be found.

Thanks be to You, O Lord, for calling out to me. I know I need to answer so that I can be rescued from the thick, high weeds of sin. I don't want to be lost and never found. Blessed be Your name for Your great love that seeks to find me. Let salvation come to my house. I will forever rejoice in Your redeeming love. In Christ's name, amen.

3

Whisper

After the earthquake came a fire, but
the LORD was not in the fire. And after
the fire came a gentle whisper.

1 KINGS 19:12 NIV

Usually when a hunter suddenly whispers to another
hunter, it's because something is happening in the
woods and their emotions have ramped up. For
example, when my son, Nathan, was about thirteen
years old, I took him deer hunting on my father-in-
law's farm in West Virginia. The difference between
this hunt and other trips he had made with me was
this was his first time to be in charge of my Marlin
.30-30 rifle.

We were walking along a ridge to a place to sit
for a while when I glimpsed two deer coming our
way. I stopped and put my hand behind my back
to give Nathan the stop-and-get-down signal. As

we slowly crouched behind a huge oak, I whispered excitedly, "Get your gun ready! Get your gun ready!"

The deer came within fifteen yards of us, but they were females. With a buck-only tag, Nathan didn't get a chance to fire the Marlin, but he's told me more than once that of all his hunting memories, this moment is one of his favorites. Hearing my sudden, breathy, adrenalin-driven command, "Get your gun ready!" resulted in his first serious case of buck fever. He says it's a feeling he fondly remembers to this day.

I can think of another fellow who well remembers hearing a whisper. In his case, the lowered voice came from God. The man's name was Elijah. He had killed a bunch of false prophets who worked for the evil king Ahab and his queen, Jezebel. The royal couple didn't like what Elijah had done, and he fled to a cave near Mount Horeb to escape their plan to kill him (see 1 Kings 19:1-8).

God instructed Elijah to leave the cave and go up the mountain. It was there that God revealed Himself to the prophet, but He didn't do it in a mighty wind or in an earthquake or in fire. Instead, it was in a "gentle blowing," a still, small voice, that

God communicated with the fleeing Elijah and instructed him on what to do to save his life.

If there was ever a time that God's people need to hear His whispers, it's now. We desperately need to know how to get through the wilderness of this darkening culture, and He alone knows the path we need to follow. We need His guidance with decisions regarding our family relationships. We need discernment when it comes to spiritual connections with those who claim to follow him. We need to know what to do with our finances. And we have a host of other extremely important matters that require God's divine directives. Without His leading, we'll be lost.

Here's a song lyric that came about as I thought about how much we all need to hear the gentle voice of our heavenly Shepherd. I have a feeling this prayer is yours as well.

Whisper

Father, in the chaos of this world and all it's
    noise
We want to hear You speaking, we need to
    hear Your voice
We don't ask for thunder or a mighty wind or
    fire

But like You did for Elijah, this is our desire
Would You
Whisper

We need to hear from You
Whisper
Just tell us what to do
Every step we take
We need You to lead the way
So to me and my brothers and my sisters
Would You whisper

From Your throne in heaven You see the
    danger up ahead
You know the way around it and how we
    must be led
But we can't hear Your warning with our
    human ears
So, Father, deep inside our spirits would You
    let us hear
Your whisper

Oh to know Your will is our mission
But we need Your grace to help us stay close
    enough to listen when You
Whisper.*

---

*   Steve Chapman, Times & Seasons Music, Inc., BMI, 2015.

4

No Other Name

There is salvation in no one else; for there
is no other name under heaven given
among men by which we must be saved.

ACTS 4:12

If a group of hunters were asked to tell which rifle
or bow they prefer, you can be sure you wouldn't
hear their preferences mentioned apologetically.
Instead, you might see some gun owner's eyes
widen with excitement as they say Remington,
Winchester, Ruger, Mossberg, Benelli, Smith &
Wesson, Henry, Marlin, or Harrington & Rich-
ardson. The archers might speak with pride about
Mathews, PSE, Parker, Hoyt, Excalibur, Ten Point,
Black Widow, Bear, Bowtech, or Diamond.

Brand names like these are spoken by hunters
with confidence because they believe in the qual-
ity they represent. The brand of a gun, for example,

can suggest valued features, such as balance and weight, stock shape and material, appearance, reliable accuracy, how it receives a scope, or how fast or flat the caliber shoots. For archers, the brand of a bow can testify to its reputation for quiet operation, how light it feels, how smooth it shoots, or how little tuning it requires.

In the way that the brand of a firearm or bow speaks of the respected and desired qualities that hunters highly regard, the name of Jesus Christ carries with it an incredible reputation that His followers gladly honor. His name refers to awesome qualities that include:

- The source of our salvation from sins
- Pure goodness
- Boundless mercy
- Complete righteousness
- Tender forgiveness
- Generous provision
- Healing for body, soul, and spirit
- Blessed hope
- Victory over death and the grave
- Abundant life

Eventually, every one alive, those who have lived, and those who are yet to be born will see and admit that Christ's name fully represents all these attributes and much more. This will be true because God Himself "highly exalted Him, and bestowed on Him the name which is above every name, so that at the name of Jesus every knee [not some knees] will [not might] bow, of those who are in heaven and on earth and under the earth, and that every tongue [not just a few] will [not possibly] confess that Jesus Christ is Lord, to the glory of God the Father" (Philippians 2:9-11).

It's by God's amazing grace that I will be among those who believe in the matchless name of the one who is worthy of all praise. Do you believe? If not, I offer the following prayer for you from Ephesians 1:18-21:

I pray that the eyes of your heart may be enlightened, so that you will know what is the hope of His calling, what are the riches of the glory of His inheritance in the saints, and what is the surpassing greatness of His power toward us who believe.

These are in accordance with the working of the strength of His might which He brought about in Christ, when He raised Him from the dead and seated Him at His right hand in the heavenly places, far above all rule and authority and power and dominion, and every name that is named, not only in this age but also in the one to come.

In the mighty name of Jesus, amen.

5

Pit Bull

We know that God causes all things to work
together for good to those who love God.

ROMANS 8:28

One of the best stories I've heard that illustrates
the truth that God works for the good of those
who love Him came from Alex Carter, a bear guide.
As we quietly talked just off Chichagof Island in
southeast Alaska, we got on the subject of dogs. I
mentioned that my daughter had been attacked by
a pit bull when she was a little girl, and Alex had
his own story about a near painful encounter with
the breed.

A few years ago I was feeling a little out of shape,
so I decided to go for a run. I was away from home,
and the little town I was in had a population of
less than a hundred people. The blacktop road I

chose to jog on had houses on each side that sat back fifty to seventy-five feet from the roadway.

The area looked run down, with rusting cars on blocks in front yards, debris around the houses, and junk littering the porches. As I trotted along, I thought, *This looks like a place where pit bulls might live.*

The thought had hardly passed when suddenly I looked to my right and saw a big pit bull running toward me down a driveway. Spit dangled from his jaws as his paws dug into the gravel. I had been running for about twenty minutes and was pretty much spent. I knew I was too tired to outrun the beast, so I decided to keep plodding along. If he attacked, then I'd do what I could to fight him off. But I whispered a prayer. *God please deliver me from this dog!*

I could hear the pit bull's nails scraping the blacktop behind me. I considered the idea of turning around suddenly and screaming at the canine demon catching up with me, and all at once I heard a thud. I slowed and turned to see the dog rolling beneath a '76 Buick on my side of the road.

Behind the wheel of the heavily built car was an elderly lady. She could hardly see over the dash, and about all I could see from where I stood were her glasses and her bluish hair. She came to a screeching halt just behind me, opened her door, got out, and walked around to the front of her tan-colored road barge to see what she had hit.

When she realized she had hit a dog, she was horrified. As the pit bull whimpered in pain and ran back toward the house where it lived, the driver finally noticed me. Surprised to see me, she said, "O my, young man. I'm so sorry I hit your dog. I didn't see it!"

I told her the dog wasn't mine. We both assumed the critter was not mortally wounded, and the elderly woman climbed back into her Buick and drove away. I sighed with relief and continued my run.

As I pounded the pavement back toward where I was staying, a chilling question came to me that I have never been able to answer to this day. *Did God send the elderly driver to save me from the pit bull or did He send the pit bull to save me from the elderly driver?* I suppose I won't know the answer until I get to heaven. All I can say is that I'm extra convinced that Romans 8:28 is true, because on that day He made all things work for the good of at least one guy who loves Him.

Dear Lord, what a wonderful promise You have given us to make sure that, whatever happens in this life, the outcome will be to the advantage of those who love You. I take comfort in both Your willingness and Your ability to do this for me and will continue to believe it's true. In Christ's name, amen.

6

Sound Above All Sounds

Suddenly there came from heaven a noise
like a violent rushing wind, and it filled the
whole house where they were sitting.

ACTS 2:2

We live about a half hour from Fort Campbell, the
home of the 101st Airborne Division, also known as
the Screaming Eagles. Because of our close proxim-
ity to the base I often get the thrill of seeing military
aircraft pass over our county as the division trains
and maintains readiness for potential missions.

It's especially exciting when I'm in the woods,
sitting in a tree stand, and suddenly the chest-
pounding sound of the rotors of a low-flying Black
Hawk helicopter chop through the air and fade
into the distance. Or maybe the earth-rumbling
roar of a huge four-engine cargo jet announces it's
coming my way. When that happens, I ignore the

world below and lift my eyes to the sky. I want to do nothing more than see the massive machine pass overhead. I anticipate that a glimpse of it will be exhilarating, and I'm always right.

When I told my dad about the air traffic around Fort Campbell, he said it reminded him of what happened years ago in our hometown, Chapmanville, West Virginia. His sister-in-law Betty was feeding her two younger brothers in the dining room, and dad joined them. Everything was normal until suddenly a deafening, wall-shaking, dish-rattling noise rattled through the house. Everyone at the table dropped their forks and ducked.

The blast lasted just a few seconds, but before quiet could return, each of them had pushed back their chairs and run out the front door to see what was behind that sound. Their neighbors were doing the same.

Those who had been outside had seen the source of the noise and reported that it came from a low-flying jet. Dad said one of his brothers was so shaken with excitement that the only thing he could say was, "Wow! This is the first time I ever saw a jet, and I didn't even see it!"

It didn't take long to learn that the pilot at the controls of the jet was a native of nearby Hamlin. His sister lived in Chapmanville and apparently was the intended recipient of the roaring prank. The pilot's name was Chuck Yeager. He not only made a lasting impression on the world of aviation, he left a legacy that lives on in the minds of a lot of people in a hollow nestled in the hills of Logan County in southern West Virginia.

That never-before-heard supersonic roar over Chapmanville is similar to what happened on the Day of Pentecost. The Lord's disciples were in prayer in the Upper Room when they suddenly heard a thunderous sound from the heavens. Scripture describes it as a rushing, mighty wind. I imagine it jolted those who heard it like that jet shook the folks in Chapmanville. For my dad and everyone else in town, the sound announced the presence of an aviation hero whose visit was memorable but momentary. But for those in the Upper Room, the great noise they heard proclaimed the arrival of the Holy Spirit of God, who came to stay.

Will there be another mighty sound from heaven? According to 1 Thessalonians 4:14-17, it will indeed happen again, and when—not if—it does, it will be a sound that will be heard far beyond the walls of any upper room or dining room. It will be so loud it will be heard worldwide by the dead and the living who believe that Jesus died and rose again. Here's how the passage describes what will happen:

> For if we believe that Jesus died and rose again, even so God will bring with Him those who have fallen asleep in Jesus. For this we say to you by the word of the Lord, that we who are alive and remain until the coming of the Lord, will not precede those who have fallen asleep. For the Lord Himself will descend from heaven with a shout, with the voice of the archangel and with the trumpet of God, and the dead in Christ will rise first. Then we who are alive and remain will be caught up together with them in the clouds to meet the Lord in the air, and so we shall always be with the Lord.

None of us know when our world will be shaken by the sound that will be heard in the heavens, but whenever it happens, I want to be one who welcomes it and doesn't dread it. Anyone who shares the sweet anticipation of that blessed noise is not frightened by the thought of it. Instead, we are consoled by it. Furthermore, in 1 Thessalonians 4:18 we are told to "comfort one another with these words."

If you believe that Jesus died and rose to redeem you from your sins and to preserve you for a place in heaven, may you be comforted by my reminder that the sound of our redemption will someday come from heaven. If you're not a believer, may the awareness of what will surely happen move you to pray the following:

Dear God, though I was not there to see it happen, I believe that Jesus died for my sins, was buried, and rose on the third day. I admit that, because of my sin, I need the redemption that is offered through Your Son's sacrifice, and I receive it with a grateful heart. From this moment on, I want to follow You. Help me to live as one who looks forward to Your coming, which will be heralded by the sound above all sounds. Thank You for accepting me into Your family. In Christ's mighty name I pray, amen.

7

True Freedom

You may eat freely.

GENESIS 2:16

To those who strongly oppose high-fence hunting, I must confess that I did it once. Here's the story:

I was excited when an invitation came to be a guest hunter on a well-known television outdoors show. Without hesitating, I accepted the offer, participated in the hunt, and arrowed a great buck on film. It was an impressive eight pointer that weighed in around 180 pounds. For me, it was my biggest deer to date. My on-camera reaction to making a quick kill shot on such a huge whitetail was wild and enthusiastic. The show host couldn't have been happier with the footage, and neither could I.

At home I continued to bask in the glow of this experience. About the time the show producer called and told me that the staff was sure the episode was going to be a favorite for their devoted viewers, I received a phone call from someone I consider to be a legend in the hunting world. I told him about the filming. He asked me where it happened. When I told him, there was a momentary silence on the other end of the line. Then the disturbing news came.

"Steve, I know about that place, and there's a lot of controversy among hunters when it comes to high-fence hunting. Some favor it, some don't have an opinion, but a whole bunch of hunters think it's not fair chase hunting and oppose it so strongly that they have no respect for hunters who kill deer inside a high fence."

I felt sick. "Are you kidding me?"

"No, I'm not. Did you not know about how opposed people can be to it?"

I wasn't aware of the controversy. I had never hunted in an enclosed area or known anyone who had. In fact, I had never heard the term "high-fence hunting" until he used it, not even when I was on location for the hunt.

I was aware there was an eleven-foot fence around the several thousand acres we were hunting, but to me the place seemed plenty big enough for any animal, including mature deer, to roam and run from danger, which they did. They had eluded me for three days before I connected.

Mark it up to naivety or ignorance, but I failed to understand the opposing views about high-fence hunting until after all was said and done. I worried that my credibility was in jeopardy and quietly hoped the footage would be mysteriously lost. But it wasn't. Instead, the prediction by the staff that it would be one of their most popular episodes came true. I bit my public-relation nails and waited.

As it turned out, to my knowledge, my appearance on the show hasn't caused the reputational damage I feared it might. Maybe the fact that the hunt was with a bow instead of a rifle on such a vast range was helpful. Or maybe not many viewers recognized the name of the place as being a fenced hunting spot. For whatever reason, I was relieved to not be inundated with sacks of hate mail or email—and I hope I don't get it now that the cat is out of the bag, or should I say, outside the fence!

My purpose for divulging the hunt inside the wall is not for arguing for or against the practice but as a helpful illustration I gleaned from the experience. I'm hopeful you'll appreciate it too, even if you're not a fan of high-fence hunting.

Even though the massive enclosure was well managed and populated with deer, there were restrictions that I had to observe as a hunter. I learned one of them when I was in a stand on the second morning. A monstrous fourteen-point buck walked under me unaware of my presence on the planet. The spread on his main beams looked wide enough for two men to stand in. I shook from head to toe with excitement until I heard a whisper from the guide sitting next to me: "You're free to shoot any buck on this property—except that one. You gotta let him walk."

Reluctantly I relaxed my grip on the mechanical string release in my right hand. I was very ready to come to a full draw, but all I was allowed to do was gawk at the incredibly huge trophy as it meandered by. In that moment I got a taste of what Adam must have felt in the Garden of Eden when God made reference to freedom for the first time. He said, "From any tree of the garden you may eat freely; but from the tree of the knowledge of good and evil you shall not eat, for in the day that you eat from it you shall surely die" (Genesis 2:16-17).

As I sat in the stand replaying the sight of the monster buck I had just seen, I silently complained about the restriction that kept me from making it my own. I knew if I were going to enjoy the rest of the hunt, I would have to focus on the freedom I had to take any other buck, not the one I couldn't take. It took some mental calisthenics to get back to a good attitude, but I managed to do it, and I'm glad I did. Besides, if I had chosen to ignore the guide's order, I would have been immediately escorted off the property and would not have been blessed with the great buck I took on camera the next day.

The first created man found out the hard way that true freedom is found in being thankful for all that he *could* have and not focus on the one thing he *couldn't* have. It's a principle that is still true to this day, and if followed, it can bring a lot of peace to anyone who understands and follows it. For example, there is a great deal of intimacy to be freely enjoyed within the bonds of marriage. But if a husband or wife is tempted by someone outside their marriage that they can't rightfully have, and they let that person become their focus, the freedom they once enjoyed is threatened. If they yield to temptation, the end result is the bondage that comes from the far-reaching effects of the sin of adultery.

The loss of freedom can also happen when gratitude for all we have is replaced by coveting something we can't have or when lust for an item we can't afford leads to stealing.

Is there a monster buck you're not allowed to have that's tempting you to disregard God's laws for right living? If so, don't forget that while you dwell in the enclosure of His grace, your freedom of heart depends on enjoying what He allows and saying no to the things He has said you can't partake of. It will help if you'll remember there's so much more to freely enjoy in this life He has given than anything He said you can't have. Be strong in saying no to it, and your reward will be great.

O God, forgive me for losing my focus on all the wonderful things You have given me and wrongly thinking about that thing You said I can't have. Thank You for enclosing me in the protection of Your marvelous grace and mercy. I want to dwell there with You all the days of my life and in the life hereafter. To Your glory and to that alone, amen.

Harmony in the Woods

Behold, how good and pleasant it is for
brothers to dwell together in unity!

PSALM 133:1

It's always an intriguing sight to see deer and turkey feeding together in the same patch of woods. While they are vastly different in that only one can fly, only one has four legs, only male turkeys grow a beard, only bucks grow antlers, and only one female of the two species lays eggs, they share a mutual interest: food.

Both like to consume various grasses and plants, but most of the time I've seen the birdy and the beast together, it's because there was a nearby acorn-bearing tree that was dropping plenty of shelled candy to the ground. Deer and turkeys love the nuts so much they'll endure each other's presence in order to partake.

I haven't seen either species fight the other over the tasty tree nuts, but I have seen them stare at each other in a way that seems to say, "I wish you would just leave!" Yet in spite of the subtle conflict that appears to exist between deer and turkeys, they feed side by side and give each other room to dine.

Imagine how much more peaceful some churches would be if their members were more like deer and turkeys. For example, if those who like singing more current worship songs would appreciate the older hymns and those who love to sing them, there'd be more harmony in the pews. If the people who prefer expository preaching would be patient with those who like topical preaching, perhaps a greater number of the congregation would be fed by the breaking of bread.

These are only two of the many areas of church life in which the saints could do better when it comes to getting along. If deer and turkeys can do it, surely the saints can. After all, whether you're a buck or a doe, a gobbler or a hen, we all love to eat from the same tree. May God help us to give each other room to enjoy what the God of the woods has to offer.

Forgive us, Lord, for being anything other than loving to one another. Thank You for providing a place called church, where such an abundance of spiritual food is served. Help us to appreciate the various ways it's presented and to always be mindful that the world will know we are Your people by the love we show to one another. In Christ's name, amen.

9

Don't Forget to Eat

Therefore I encourage you to take some
food, for this is your preservation.

ACTS 27:34

Just before Annie left with our daughter, Heidi, for
a five-day, girls-only trip, she reminded me about
the food she had made for me and stored in the
refrigerator. The list included her awesome venison chili, a chicken casserole, slaw, peas, fresh salsa,
precooked oatmeal for breakfast, and a stash of
peanut butter cookies.

As we hugged good-bye, she lovingly put her finger on my chest and said, "I know you better than
you know yourself. When your mind gets going in
one direction and you start doing something, you
forget to eat. I personally don't understand how
anyone can do such a thing, and in fact, you're the
only person I know on the entire planet who can go

all day long and never give a thought to food. You need your strength, so promise me you'll eat."

I comforted my wife with a guarantee that I would do my best to not let all her cooking be done in vain. Then she added a footnote to her request that confirmed she did indeed know me very well.

"I know it's deer season, and this evening you'll probably go over to the Walker farm and climb up a tree. If you do, make sure you've fed yourself. The last thing I want to hear is that you passed out from malnourishment and fell out of your stand. If you die that way, I'll have to kill you!"

I smiled, knowing that even though she tempered her demand with humor, she was serious. We kissed and she drove away with my assurance that I wouldn't ignore her wishes. Ten minutes later I was headed down a single-lane road in my mind.

I went straight to the garage and got my crossbow out to do some practice shooting. Thirty minutes later I was doing another thing I had to do, and then another, and by two o'clock that afternoon I was gathering my gear to head to the deer stand. That's when I heard Annie's words echo in my head: "Promise me you'll eat!"

Sure enough, just like Annie had pointed out, I had forgotten to feed myself. Not wanting to disappoint my bride or, worse, let her hear that I was found hanging lifelessly at the end of my safety harness, I warmed up some chili and chowed down. I actually felt stronger when I headed to the woods and wondered why I hadn't eaten earlier. I appreciated that Annie's love for me extended to my belly. I'm a blessed man.

If you've ever read Acts 27, you know that Annie is not the only one concerned about someone eating. The apostle Paul was a prisoner on a ship with 275 other people and sailing to Rome. They ran into all kinds of trouble that hindered them from reaching their destination, and they transferred to another ship that also faced bad weather. Paul warned the sailors that they were headed into great danger, but they didn't listen.

Finally, after two weeks of intensely rough sailing and knowing they were going to lose the ship, he said, "'Today is the fourteenth day that you have been constantly watching and going without eating, having taken nothing. Therefore I encourage you to take some food, for this is for your preservation, for not a hair from the head of any of you will perish.' Having said this, he took bread and gave thanks to God in the presence of all, and he broke it and began to eat. All of them were encouraged and they themselves also took food" (Acts 27:33-36).

As it turned out, the ship struck a reef, ran aground, and broke up. But all 276 people lived through the wreck. Some of them had to swim, and some paddled on planks and other debris from the ship. Had they not eaten, the outcome could have been far worse.

Annie's urging me to eat and Paul's warning to his fellow travelers to do the same are great illustrations of what God would have us do spiritually. So many of us get distracted by everyday life and our daily struggles and fail to take in enough nourishment to help us endure what's ahead. When this happens, the result is weakness that causes us to tremble and give in to doubt and fear. Then we wonder why we can't make any progress in our spiritual work or warfare.

Paul said, "Take some food, for this is your preservation," and gave the others a guarantee: "For not a hair from the head of any of you will perish." And his promise was proven true. It's one you can count on today. So if you've forgotten to eat or have been distracted by the rough seas of life, it's time to listen to what Paul—and Annie—said to do. "Eat!"

God, I come to You with thanks for the provision of the Bread of Life that You offer through Your written Word. I will eat in spite of any lack of appetite, because I know I need the strength it gives for the journey. In Christ's name, amen.

10

Yes, but Not Yet

You shall hear of wars and rumors of wars: see
that you be not troubled: for all these things
must come to pass, but the end is not yet.

MATTHEW 24:6 KJV 2000e

One of my favorite movie moments is in *Gladiator*, starring Russell Crowe. Playing the role of a Roman general named Maximus, his loyalty gained him favor from the emperor, Marcus Aurelius. His skills as a warrior and leader were well known and respected but posed a dreaded problem for him: his wish to retire and return home to his wife and son was delayed when the emperor told him he was needed to lead one more battle.

Enter the emperor's jealous son, Commodus, played by Joaquin Phoenix. His hatred of the favored general and his unbridled ambition to become emperor drove him to murder his father and condemn Maximus to slavery. The general's unfortunate fate landed him in the ranks of gladiators and farther away from his home.

As a mighty fighter, Maximus rose through the ranks of those who were thrown into the arena. His victories gained the favor of the crowds, but as his fame grew so did his sadness. He spent his quiet moments in the dark, dingy rooms beneath the floor of the arena longing desperately to be reunited with his wife and son.

Maximus found a close friend in another gladiator, Juba, played by Djimon Hounsou. Juba recognized Maximus's deeply strong feelings about getting back to his family because he hoped for the same. In a very emotional scene where the two of them share their thoughts about their loved ones back home, Maximus asked if it would ever happen. Juba looked at his friend with a reassuring smile and said what I consider to be one of the greatest lines ever penned for a movie script.

"You will meet them again. But not yet. Not yet."

By themselves, the two words, *not yet*, don't pack much of a punch. But because they are placed against the backdrop of the shared hopes of two desperately homesick men, I felt their impact.

Since I watched *Gladiator* several years ago, it's hard to tell how many times I've used those two words from Juba's line. I even try to smile like he did when he said them. Here are a few examples of usage...

- A friend asks, "Has your new grandbaby arrived?" I smile and answer, "Not yet."

- Annie asks, "Have you saved up enough to get your new tractor?" (smile) "Not yet."

- While waiting anxiously for a massive Montana bull elk to feed into the range of my rifle I nervously grin and silently coach myself, *not yet*.

Of course, the most anticipated event ahead for all of us is written about in Matthew 24:1-6. As ominous sounding as the passage is, notice how it ends:

Jesus went out, and departed from the temple: and his disciples came to him to show him the buildings of the temple. And Jesus said unto them,

See you not all these things? verily I say unto you, There shall not be left here one stone upon another, that shall not be thrown down. And as he sat upon the mount of Olives, the disciples came unto him privately, saying, Tell us, when shall these things be? and what shall be the sign of your coming, and of the end of the world? And Jesus answered and said unto them, Take heed that no man deceive you. For many shall come in my name, saying, I am Christ; and shall deceive many. And you shall hear of wars and rumors of wars: see that you be not troubled: for all these things must come to pass, but the end is *not yet* (KJV 2000e, emphasis added).

I wonder if a comforting smile came to the face of Jesus when He got to the last line of this statement. Surely His followers were encouraged when they heard Him say that an end to the trouble would come. I know I certainly take comfort in them.

Paul echoed that hope: "The creation itself also will be set free from its slavery to corruption into the freedom of the glory of the children of God." (Romans 8:21).

Knowing that God will deliver His people from the bonds of this world and will eventually bring us home to heaven are the hopes that keep me pressing on. Perhaps you feel the same. If so, Paul talked about people like us when he said to Timothy, "The victor's crown of righteousness is now waiting for me, which the Lord, the righteous Judge, will give to me on the day that he comes, and not only to me but also to all who eagerly wait for his appearing" (2 Timothy 4:8 ISV).

When you start to wonder if it will ever happen, just remember, it will, but *not yet*!

Oh God, You know very well that the cares of this life and the suffering it can bring can often make me feel like a slave to this world. It's in those times that it's so hard to trust that You will come as promised and deliver me from this bondage. When I question if that day will come, help me to remember that You've already provided the encouragement and comfort that I need when you said, "The end is not yet."

11

If'n You Ain't fir 'Im

He who is not with Me is against Me; and
he who does not gather with Me scatters.

MATTHEW 12:30

When I drive north from Tennessee to hunt deer or
turkey with my friend in Indiana, the trip includes
a two-hour drive through Kentucky. During that
time I like to listen to the radio because of the style
of music that seems plentiful in the area. Suffice it
to say, there's more than one reason they call it the
Bluegrass State.

The stations that feature traditional bluegrass
that I most enjoy are not the slick, professionally
produced, nationally syndicated FM broadcasts.
Instead, it's the local talent that can be heard on the
AM stations.

I especially enjoy shows that feature live, in-
studio performances. The playing may not always

be spot-on perfect, and the mix might not be a stellar blend of instrumentals and vocals, but the sound is raw and real. Plus there's another aspect of the live shows that can be very entertaining: the talking.

Very often the musically talented folks who gather around the microphones in a radio station studio come from rural communities, where the dialogue is homespun. Country drawls are a sweet sound to my ear. When they talk, I feel like I'm listening to family.

On a down-home program you can hear unforgettable statements that are not only unique but jam-packed with truth. One is especially memorable because of the voice tone of the one delivering the quip.

Before launching into a bluegrass version of "The Old Rugged Cross," a tenor spoke up with his unusually high-pitched voice. "Here's a requested number that we wanna send out to my Grannie. If she was here today, she'd tell you what she's told me all my life. 'When it comes to Jesus, "If'n you ain't fir 'im, you're agin 'im."'"

A round of amens came from the group members, and then the banjo player kicked off the intro in a medium tempo and away they went. I didn't dare turn the radio dial. I stayed tuned for the rest of the half-hour show. When it ended with an instrumental version of "There's Room at the Cross for You," the tenor's voice broke in once more, and he said in his very countrified way, "To everyone out there in radio land, don't firget what my Grannie said, 'When it comes to Jesus, if'n you ain't fir 'im, you're agin 'im!'"

The tenor's parting message not only deserves a big amen from me, but it also is worthy of passing on to others. So I ask you, when it comes to Jesus, are you fir 'im or agin 'im?

Lord, I thank You for Your grace that drew me into a relationship with You. It is a blessing beyond measure to be on Your side. I know it's where I'll be safe and it's where my soul can rest. I trust You to show me any place in my heart that is not fully for You. May it be so until all that will not praise You is undone. In the sweet name of Jesus, I pray, amen.

12

God's Not Through with Her Yet

Joshua was old and advanced in years when the LORD said to him, "You are old and advanced in years, and very much of the land remains to be possessed."

JOSHUA 13:1

When I sit quietly for an hour or three in a tree stand or as motionless as possible while perched on my three-legged ground stool, I know what's coming when I stand up to leave. Every muscle and joint in my body is going to protest the pain that comes from inactivity. The only thing I've found that helps to dismiss the aches is to grunt, and lately I've been doing more and more grunting. Each time it reminds me that I'm facing the winter of my years, which means there are fewer days before than there are behind me. While it's the normal course of things, it doesn't mean I like the idea.

Dealing with the reality that I have an expiration date stamped on me somewhere is a bit disconcerting, but one thing that gives me comfort is that God has the date perfectly timed. It will come when He determines that my purpose for being here is completed. Until then, I want to be busy doing whatever He asks and be content with wherever He wants me to do it.

There are those who have exemplified a great attitude about aging who I look to for inspiration. Like the woman in the following story, I want to be available to be used by the Lord until my clock winds completely down.

God's Not Through with Her Yet

She's in a home, room forty-eight
She'll turn ninety come next May
It's been a while since I was there
I went to show her that I still care
I thought I'd find her sitting alone
Nothing to do, but I was wrong
When I walked in, she said, "Come with me

Gotta help someone in room thirty-three!"

She's got friends who need her to pray
And hear her sing "Amazing Grace"
To sit a while and read the Bible by their bed
She's got stories they want to hear
To help them remember the Lord is near
Oh, it's clear to me, God's not through with
     her yet

So I walked with her down the hall
I was amazed at what I saw
Just like an angel sent from above
She dried their tears and showed God's love
Then she smiled and took their hand
To let them know they had a friend
And on our way back to her room
She said, "So little time and so much to do."

Then we said good-bye, and I whispered as I
     turned to leave
Lord, just like You've done with her, always
     use me.*

---

*   Steve Chapman and Tim Morgan, Times & Seasons Music, BMI,
Mathis Mountain Music (LLC), 2015.

Loving and merciful God who knows the number of my days, I ask that You will make me useful for as long as I inhabit this temporal body. Reveal the purpose that You have for me and grant me strength and wisdom to do whatever You desire for me to do. Thank You for the opportunity to serve You by serving others. May they see Your grace as I perform the tasks You set before me so they will give You, and You alone, all the glory. In Christ's name I pray, amen.

13

I Need More Light

Jesus said, "Are you still lacking
in understanding also?"

MATTHEW 15:16

My friend Joe has a farm that I've hunted more
than any place in the last several years. There is
a specific patch of woods I especially love to deer
hunt because the oak trees there are laden with
acorns almost every season.

One day I arrived at Joe's place well before
dawn to bow hunt for deer in a permanently
mounted lock-on-type tree stand. The placement
was between two heavily used trails that merged
ten yards beyond. With shooting light still about
twenty minutes away, the interior of the woods was
pitch black. I knew the darkness would linger due
to the heavy late-September foliage that blocked
the morning sunlight.

As I sat staring at what appeared to be the inside of an abandoned coal mine, I heard the faint sound of a familiar crunch in the leaves behind me. Something weighty was moving through the woods.

I slowly slid my right hand to my left wrist to feel for my watch. Through the thin cloth of the glove that covered the tip of my index finger I felt the button that would light up the watch face. I guessed it was about twenty-five minutes before I could legally come to full draw.

Ten minutes later I still heard small steps in the woods. I was sure it was a deer feeding on fresh, abundant white oak acorns. My hope was that the feast would keep the deer browsing in that spot long enough for sunrise to come.

After ten minutes passed, the crunch in the leaves became the sound of teeth crunching on hard acorn shells. Because it seemed to be a lone deer, I assumed a buck had come in close. Needless to say, adrenalin was flowing in my body like water through a garden hose.

Finally, through small openings in the tree canopy above, I could see the sky slowly turn from black to gray, but the silhouette of the leaves was the only shape I could clearly see. Not much was identifiable inside the woods. And then the deer meandered over to feed on the nuts around the tree next to my stand. I could hear steps right below me, but because I was sixteen feet above the ground, I couldn't clearly make out the shape of its body.

The wind carried my scent away from the deer, otherwise I would have already been busted. For another three or four minutes the animal fed below me, long enough for the woods to gain just a little light. I remained seated, raised my bow, and held it out in front of me. I tried to see my fifteen-yard pin at arm's length in the dim light, but it was not there. There was no way to take a legal shot.

As if I could speed up the arrival of dawn, I kept whispering, "I need more light. C'mon. Just a little more!" Neither the sun nor the planet cooperated. It felt like a full week had passed, but finally enough light filled the area around me that I wouldn't break a law if I shot. But by that time the deer, a really nice buck, had wandered out of range. I could see him standing about fifty yards away, still munching on his nutty breakfast.

I didn't take a deer off of Joe's farm that day, but

the memory of how hard I wished, even prayed, for the light to hurry up and help me out has crossed my mind quite often, especially when I've struggled to understand something that has me stumped. Sometimes it was a biblical truth I couldn't seem to grasp or when I tried to figure out why someone did something strange or I needed wisdom about a an important, life-changing decision.

In times like these I know I have to be as willing to admit my need for understanding as Peter was after he heard Jesus say of the hypocritical Pharisees, "It is not what enters into the mouth that defiles the man, but what proceeds out of the mouth, this defiles the man" (Matthew 15:11). The illustration went right over Peter's head, because he said, "Explain the parable to us" (verse 15). Apparently, by saying "to us" meant that Peter wasn't alone in needing the light of understanding.

Jesus must have expected his disciples to be astute enough to get the gist of what His metaphor meant, because He responded with a question that contained a gentle rebuke: "Are you still lacking in understanding also?" (verse 16). Though seemingly concerned about their inability to understand what He'd said, with the patience of a gentle shepherd, Jesus helped Peter and the others to understand what He meant.

Just like I kept saying while I was hunting at Joe's farm, "I need more light," I remain willing to say it when I need understanding in regard to matters beyond the hunter's woods. Thankfully, I have a promise in James 1:5 that God will provide the needed light. The promise is yours too. All we have to do is ask!

> If any of you lacks wisdom, let him ask of God, who gives to all generously and without reproach, and it will be given to him. But he must ask in faith without any doubting (James 1:5-6).

Oh God, too many times in the past I've needed wisdom but didn't realize I could ask You for it. I don't want to lean on my own understanding, because the outcome is never good. Help me to always admit my need for Your light and to wait on You to give it. I want to do this so I can walk in the path You have set before me. In the bright and shining name of Jesus, amen.

14

Rearview Mirror

The LORD is near to the brokenhearted and
saves those who are crushed in spirit.

PSALM 34:18

When Nathan was a teenager I took him and one
of his friends to a Midwestern state to hunt whitetails. They sat in the backseat and talked ten miles
a minute. It was enjoyable to hear their discussions
about girls, music, food, girls, food, and music.

When I joined in the conversation to discuss
where we'd be hunting, I remember looking at our
guest in the rearview mirror. When his eyes met
mine, I could see the excitement in them. He was
pumped about the two days of hunting ahead of us,
and his enthusiasm was a delight to see.

I also recall quietly thinking about the fact that
this young man didn't have a dad on the hunt. He
was fatherless. It was a fact he never mentioned

during our time together, but I wondered if he thought about it.

None of us got a deer during the hunt, but we bagged some really fun stories to tell later. I didn't realize at first how much tighter our guest held the memory of this trip than Nathan and I did. He often talked especially to me about it, which made me wonder if he did because of how rare it was for him to be with a dad, even if it wasn't his own.

I learned later I was right about the boy's need to fill a father void in his soul. I did what I could to span the gap, but I was aware that ultimately I couldn't meet his need. I watched him struggle through life, making decisions that seemed to work against him more than for him. My heart ached as he searched for a path to peace and contentment. I'm not sure either of those goals were ever reached.

I've often thought about that young man, particularly the moment he and I connected in the rearview mirror on our way to the deer hunt. I wondered how many times that visual connection might have happened with him and his dad before his parents' divorce, and if it did, what did it mean to both of them now. With that imagery in mind, I wrote the following song lyric to help others understand what the journey of a fatherless boy can look like.

Rearview Mirror

I was just a kid in the backseat
Riding with my father
I saw him look at me in the rearview mirror
I didn't know what he was thinking
How am I gonna tell that boy that I'll be
*   leaving*
He just went away, and since that day
The road of life ain't been easy
I try moving on but the memories keep me
Wishing for what I didn't have
Missing all the right turns cause I was looking
     back
To see his eyes
Ain't no way to drive
In that rearview mirror

I wonder if he knew that just a phone call
Maybe just a letter
To say it wasn't my fault might have made it
     better

Sometimes I imagine he's somewhere on a
     highway
He can't see where he's going cause he sees my
     face
Through the tears, through the years

I was just a kid in the backseat
Riding with my father
I saw him look at me in that rearview mirror.*

If you see yourself in this story, either as the kid
or the dad, no doubt it brings up some feelings that
are hard to face. Whether you're the son or daughter who feels abandoned or you're the one who feels
the remorse and regret of leaving, I hope you'll take
comfort in the words of Psalm 34:18: "The LORD is
near to the brokenhearted and saves those who are
crushed in spirit."

Prayer of an abandoned child:

Father in heaven, You know how difficult it is
for me to call You Father. Yet I do it now because
I trust Your mercy extends even to me. I ask You

---

*   Steve Chapman, Times & Seasons Music, Inc., BMI, 2015.

to show me what You mean by Your promise to be "near to the brokenhearted." I'm certainly one of those whose heart has been crushed by sad circumstances. I keep trying to drive on the road of time while looking at my past through the rearview mirror, and all I seem to do is run off the road. I need Your presence in my life to help me look forward. From this day on, guide me, teach me, hunt with me, fish with me through whatever means You choose. Reveal Your Fatherhood to me. I want to know You as my Dad, my Abba Father. May it be so in the name of Your Son, my Redeemer, Lord, and Brother, Christ Jesus, amen.

Prayer of the parent who left:

O merciful Father in heaven, I bring to You my sincere regret for the decisions I've made that have hurt my child. I thought I could move on and forget their pain, but their wounds are added to my own. Please forgive me and help me to see clearly what I can do to bring some healing to their life and to mine. I pray for the courage to make a call or write a letter or arrange a visit and the wisdom for what to say. Thank You for Your grace that reaches even to the loneliest highway and comforts my soul with the promise that You will be near broken hearts like mine and my child's. Blessed be the name of Jesus, in which I pray, amen.

15

The Inconvenience of Sin

Even as they did not like to retain God
in their knowledge, God gave them
over to a reprobate mind, to do those
things which are not convenient.

ROMANS 1:28 KJV

Leaning on the statute of limitations for a pardon and confessing ignorance, I now admit to wrong-doing in 1963. I had just been introduced to hunting in the fall of my twelfth year and was so captivated by it that when the season ended, I wasn't sure I could wait until the next October to carry a gun into the woods. Springtime came with an opportunity I didn't expect.

A friend of my father invited me to come to his farm and hunt groundhogs. He loaned me a Winchester .30-30 with open sights to use on the furry crop-eating burrowers. On the first morning I went out, I connected with a couple of them.

I had walked all afternoon on the property and decided to take five. I found a huge cedar tree in the middle of a ten-acre field. As I sat there I watched for groundhogs that might show themselves in the short grass, but something else caught my eye.

At the far end of the field a brown spot appeared, and it was much larger than a groundhog. I squinted, and after studying the shape for a half minute I realized it was a deer.

I had never seen a whitetail in my short experience as a hunter because they were rare in that area in the 1960s. All I had hunted in my first season were plentiful squirrels. So when I sighted the lone deer in the distance, I was so excited that every other thought dropped out of my mind but one: *shoot that deer.* There were no questions in my mind at all, such as, *Is there a law against this? Is this right?* All I had was an answer.

Boom!

I immediately looked over the barrel after the shot and saw dirt fly up about ten yards in front of the deer. It flinched and then went back to feeding.

I couldn't believe the blast of the .30-30 didn't make it run into the brush at the edge of the field.

My heart was pumping like the number-one piston in a full-out Dodge 440 engine as I quickly levered another cartridge and took aim. This time I put the bead above the back of the deer. With open sights I couldn't tell exactly how far above its shoulder I was aiming, but I held steady and pulled the trigger. I saw the deer kick high with its hind legs and then dart into the brush.

I didn't know that the animal's kicking motion was a telltale sign that it had been hit. I assumed I had only scared it because it ran away. But I thought I'd at least head into the thicket where I last saw it and maybe get another chance to shoot.

I walked to the field edge and found ivy covering the ground where the deer had entered the brush. I stepped high through it and came to an opening where I could see clearly inside the thicket.

"What?" I said full voice because I was shocked. The deer lay dead less than fifteen yards ahead of me. I stood for a moment and watched to see if there was any movement. There was none. I walked toward it and dropped to my knees next to the lifeless body. Feeling very stunned, I just looked at it from end to end. It was my first deer.

A minute or two passed as I processed a mixture of emotions. It was surreal to be that close to such a huge animal. Reality returned with the thought, *Now what do I do?* I realized there was only one option. I had to go back to the house of the man who had invited me to chase groundhogs and tell him about the deer.

When I sat down at his kitchen table, he told me he had heard my shots and asked how many groundhogs I had gotten for him. I told him about two I had shot but felt nervous knowing I had one more detail to report. I thought about keeping the deer kill to myself, but I couldn't do it. I just blurted it out.

"Uh, by the way, I killed a deer!"

Things got really quiet for a few seconds except for the tapping of his fingers on the table. Then he said, "Well, deer aren't in season right now, so we got us a problem on our hands. We can't waste the meat. That would be worse than the wrong thing you've done."

It was at that moment I fully realized I had

made a terrible mistake. I felt awful and apologized. I waited to hear what his plan was.

"Dark is not that far away, and its cool enough that the meat won't spoil. We'll have to wait till the sun is down and go get the deer. I have a neighbor who will really appreciate the meat. But I'll warn you, doing what we gotta do after dark won't be convenient like it would be in the daylight."

In order to not risk anyone seeing us in the woods at night, we didn't use a flashlight to get to the deer. Instead we stumbled through and risked falling and hurting ourselves. Once we got to the carcass, the field dressing process was more difficult in the dim light of the moon. Then dragging the deer through the woods up and down a few hollows instead of driving to get it with a noisy tractor resulted in some backbreaking work. The only redeemable thing that came of it was that a nearby family unexpectedly received about fifty pounds of edible venison.

I regret my hunting transgression and repented long ago. I hope my fellow hunters who have heard my confession are as forgiving as the Lord is. At the least I learned one good lesson. The farmer was right, there's nothing convenient about doing wrong.

In my case, breaking the law by killing a deer out of season resulted in having to complete the harvest in a very cumbersome and impractical way. Worse yet, my wrongdoing put the landowner in a very awkward position. Unfortunately, these aren't the only things I've done in the past that prove the truth that sin is never convenient. Having to find places to hide in order to do drugs, driving a hundred miles out of my way to avoid the embarrassment of being recognized when buying something that was not godly, and the messy tactic of keeping track of lies in order to hide a truth are just a few.

I'm not saying I have attained perfection, but thankfully God in His great compassion for sinners redeemed me years ago and opened my eyes to how much more convenient living honest can be. It's an advantage that benefits my life in a lot of ways. For example, being faithful to my wife doesn't require the constant concealment of secrets. Not partaking of alcohol or other mind-altering substances means I don't have to chase the next drink or the next pill. Avoiding being deceitful with money means I don't have to spend my time figuring out ways to cheat someone. It's simply a more practical way of living.

Have you figured out that sin is always the inconvenient choice? If not, I hope you will. If you'll stop and think about how much energy it requires to transgress, I think you'll agree that living righteously will save you time, heartache, work, and even money.

Dear God, forgive me for those things I've done that are inconvenient, impractical, and improper. I don't want to do them any longer. Instead, I want my mind and heart to be committed to knowing You and the ways You have asked me to live. Please show me how to avoid doing things that will cost me strength that could be used to Your glory. Blessed be Your name for the help You give. In Christ's name I pray, amen.

16

If You're Breathing You're Busted

Let your speech always be with grace.

COLOSSIANS 4:6

When I flew three states away for a midwinter archery deer hunt with a friend, he met me at baggage claim and helped me with my luggage. As he dragged my heavy gear case off the conveyor, he moaned and said, "Good grief, I didn't know you were bringing a four-wheeler with you!"

"Really, Steve," he said, "what all's in this case?"

As I retrieved my bow case, I said, "Two sets of camo, boots, coats, long johns, hats, socks, Skivvies, safety harness, cameras—do you want me to go on?"

"There's more?"

"Oh yes. I brought my arm guard, my string

release, plus a spare just in case, an extra set of broadheads, binoculars, scent-free soap and shampoo, bottle of scent cover spray, and—"

My friend stopped me. "Okay. I can understand you bringing all the stuff you mentioned. Your packing list sounds like mine, but I can tell you this. You wasted your money on the cover spray."

In an effort to defend the purchase and usage of the large container of the scent suppression product, I said, "Hey man, I'm a real stickler for being as undetectable by a deer's nose as I can be. Do you not use the stuff?"

"No way. I'd rather spend my cash on something else I need—like arrows." Then he said something that made a ton of sense.

"I definitely recommend using scent-free laundry detergent and shampoo, but as far as the scent spray goes, I'm not convinced it's worth the investment. Here's the deal—if you're breathing, you're busted. The human mouth is host to hundreds of different types of bacteria that produce various sulfur-based odors. As long as you exhale you're leaving plenty of evidence of your presence in the air. Don't think for a minute a deer can't smell it."

He'd made a good point, so I asked, "What do you suggest?"

"Neutral-smelling clothes, hunt facing the wind, and apple slices."

"Apple slices?"

"Yep. Suck on an apple slice. Not only will it sweeten your breath, they're a whole lot cheaper than scent spray. And they taste a lot better too!"

From that day to this one, I've rarely deer hunted without an apple in my pack. I feel much more hopeful about outsmarting the nose of a deer when my breath is laden with apple molecules. In fact, I'm convinced it's one of the main reasons a mainframe ten-pointer came within ten yards of me one morning without getting spooked. I was worried that the high-pressure weather system that was pushing the air to the ground around my stand would carry my scent to him, but thanks to my well-prepared camo and the added advantage of my apple breath, his rack is now in my possession.

Whenever I'm around deer and I break out my Ziploc bag of Gala slices, my purpose is to not offend them with my breath. When it comes to being around people, I hope to do the same thing, but in more ways than one. Physically, to avoid breath so foul that it would make someone run away, I try to always keep some gum or mints handy.

Spiritually, I've found that the Word of God does the most to freshen my mouth so I don't offend anyone. His Word can eliminate the foul smell of gossip, slander, insults, and other personality *dis-odors* that can be sickening to anyone who gets a whiff of them.

As an example of what speech smells like after it's been freshened by God's Word, consider what the Lord told Moses to say to Aaron and his sons in Numbers 6:23-26: "You shall bless the sons of Israel. You shall say to them: The Lord bless you, and keep you; the Lord make His face shine on you, and be gracious to you; the Lord lift up His countenance on you, and give you peace."

The aroma of words like these is sweet, indeed, and there's more where they came from. Like a Ziploc bag of apple slices, the Bible is filled with words that can make your speech a blessing. Using both is a very good idea, because whether you're in a deer stand or in a crowded room, if you're breathing, you're busted.

God, I know that the most effective way to spiritually freshen my breath is to keep Your written Word in my mouth. I don't want my conversation to be offensive to others. I want to give them the blessing of Your grace instead. I ask You to help me do this daily in the name of Your sweet Son, Jesus, amen.

17

The Ear Will Appear

Blessed be the God and Father
of our Lord Jesus Christ, who has
blessed us with every spiritual blessing in the heavenly places in Christ.

Ephesians 1:3

One of the farms where I enjoy hunting belongs to
a neighbor who lives on a back road only two miles
from our house. Because I walk four miles every
other day (I skip a day to allow my aging joints to
heal), I go right by it often.

One of the things I especially like about the
farm is that there are either soybeans or corn growing in the fields. While the crops represent a cash
flow for the owner, for me it means the critters will
hang around because of the food source.

One year the corn crop was doing especially
well. I had heard that when it comes to gauging

the progress of a corn crop, the rule of thumb is *knee high by the Fourth of July*. If that were the case, then the stalks were way ahead of schedule, because in mid-June the tops were shoulder high. But as tall as they were, something about them caught my attention.

There were plenty of luscious leaves, and the height and width of the stalks suggested they were able to support some ears, but none were popping through. The fruit of the stalk was in there, no doubt. It was just a matter of time before their appearance. I knew it wouldn't be long until whitetail would be sneaking in and enjoying the bounty.

As I walked by and looked at one earless stalk after another, I realized I was looking at an illustration of Ephesians 1:3: "Blessed be the God and Father of our Lord Jesus Christ, who has blessed us with every spiritual blessing in the heavenly places in Christ."

While the cornstalks were not quite mature enough to produce fruit, they already contained everything they needed to do so. They didn't have to force the fruit to appear; they just had to stay rooted in the ground.

In the same way, believers in Christ have been given everything needed to eventually yield the fruit of love, joy, peace, patience, kindness, goodness, faithfulness, gentleness, and self-control (see Galatians 5:22-23). It happened when we were planted in Christ. Given a chance to grow and mature, we will yield a crop we—as well as those around us—can enjoy.

Father in heaven, thank You for placing in my spirit all the necessary ingredients I need to bear fruit for You. You did it the day I came to You in repentance of my transgressions and began to live for You. Help me to rest in the knowledge that I will bear fruit as You feed me with the nutrients that come from the rich soil of Your Word. I want that to happen to Your glory and that alone. In the name of Jesus, amen.

18

Out of the Comfort Zone

Peter got out of the boat, and walked on
the water and came toward Jesus.

MATTHEW 14:29

During a self-guided elk hunt in Colorado and well
before daylight, my friend Don and I parked our
four-wheeler along a high trail and walked into a
deep canyon. When we got to the bottom, Don
took a stand along a beautiful creek bed where we
had seen elk sign the day before. I went about three
hundred yards farther south to sit for a while and
watch a stand of aspens.

After a couple of hours of not seeing any elk
move through the area, I decided to go to the opposite side of the valley and check it out. I had no idea
what the lay of the land was, but I began the climb.

About thirty minutes later I was standing on
a flat well above the creek bed. The area held a

network of trails made by elk as well as mule deer. I quietly followed one of the more used trails through some tall, fully leafed saplings, and all of a sudden two words crossed my mind: mountain lion. That thought left me feeling very uncomfortable.

The what-ifs that came to mind with those two words were chilling. What if I see one? What if he attacks? What if Don doesn't hear me when I scream for help? What if I'm seriously hurt—will they ever find me?

I knew the mental road of fear that I ran down as I stood motionless on that flat would lead me into an emotional pit where I would lose all the enjoyment of where I was and what I was doing. For that reason I forced myself to stop the what-if-ing in order to regain some peace. I saw a huge rock that overlooked the area and headed to it.

From that perch, about twenty minutes later, I glimpsed a cow elk moving slowly through the aspens on the other side of the flat. I watched her for about thirty seconds but had no chance for a sure shot through the trees. Then she was gone. I didn't experience the thrill of filling my cow tag, but at least I had a sense of gratification that by risking a move to a different spot, as nerve testing as it was, I had enjoyed a visual of a Rocky Mountain elk. As it turned out, it was the only one I saw the five days I was there.

A couple of years later I recalled that morning in Colorado when I was in church. (Yes, I enjoyed a hunting memory while the preacher was preaching. Forgive me.) The pastor told the story of Peter's getting out of the safety of the boat and taking a brief walk of faith on the Sea of Galilee. He said, "If a believer never steps out of their comfort zone, they're missing a great opportunity to see God do something wonderful."

His context was a young woman who, in spite of her normally reserved personality, went as a missionary to a predominantly Muslim region to share the gospel of Christ. He told of some amazing results of her work and how brave it was of her to step out of the comfort zone of her quiet life in America.

Using her story as a backdrop, the pastor challenged us to share the gospel even if it required us to step out of our comfort zone. For some, the place they feel comfortable is not speaking publicly or initiating conversations. For others, they never do anything that could result in rejection. Then he mentioned the comfort and convenience of the cozy towns and neighborhoods in which we lived might be tough for some folks to forsake.

As I listened I realized that what I did in that Colorado valley was a picture of what I was being encouraged to do by the pastor. In the vast territory around me, I left the comfort of being near my buddy and ventured to a place where I didn't feel all that comfy! Yet had I not done it, I would not have had the exhilaration of seeing an elk. Of course neither the experience nor the result was as significant as that of the young missionary in a Muslim community, but at least it helped me to get a good handle on what the preacher was encouraging us to do.

Whether the mission field is at home, at work, at school, on the street, at a restaurant, in a mall, or on the other side of the world, if getting there and sharing our faith requires stepping out of our comfort zone, it might not be easy, but it can potentially make a huge eternal difference in someone's life if they yield it to the Savior.

Lord, like Your servant Peter, who was brave enough to step out of the safety and comfort of the boat and walk toward You, I want to be willing to walk outside of my comfort zone to tell others about You. Forgive me for those times I've yielded to my fears and not seized an opportunity to speak about You. Help me from this day forward to step out for You in faith and share Your love. In Your name I pray, amen.

19

Right Now

Day and night they never cease to say,
"Holy, holy, holy, is the Lord God, the
Almighty, who was and is and is to come."

REVELATION 4:8 ESV

I called a friend around 10:30 a.m. to see if he might have time to go turkey hunting with me at a neighbor's farm the next morning. He agreed to go, and before we hung up, he said, "Sure wish we could be out there today 'cause you know what they're doing right now, don't you?" And I did indeed know what he was referring to.

"Yep. I thought about that. Right now the big boys are probably walking around in the upper field, looking for love and yelling their big white heads off. It hurts to think about it, but tomorrow they'll likely be at it again. They seem to always be there!"

Both of us ached having to wait several hours to hunt. We set a time to meet before daylight the next day, and when I hung up the phone I chuckled at how both of us were thinking about the same thing, namely, what the gobblers were doing even though we weren't there to see it.

Speaking of something that's going on right now even though you and I are not there to see it, consider the following passage:

> Around the throne, on each side of the throne, are four living creatures, full of eyes in front and behind: the first living creature like a lion, the second living creature like an ox, the third living creature with the face of a man, and the fourth living creature like an eagle in flight. And the four living creatures, each of them with six wings, are full of eyes all around and within, and day and night they never cease to say,

> "Holy, holy, holy, is the Lord God Almighty,
>   who was and is and is to come!"

> And whenever the living creatures give glory and honor and thanks to him who is seated on the

throne, who lives forever and ever, the twenty-four elders fall down before him who is seated on the throne and worship him who lives forever and ever. They cast their crowns before the throne, saying,

> "Worthy are you, our Lord and God,
>> to receive glory and honor and power,
> for you created all things,
>> and by your will they existed and were
> created" (Revelation 4:6-11 ESV).

It's simply amazing to realize that right now, at this very moment, as you read this page, the worship of God as described in Revelation 4 is happening. The praise due Him doesn't start when the countdown on overhead screens at the front of church sanctuaries reaches zero on Sunday morning. It doesn't start when we put a worship disk in a player and push Play or log on to a favorite worship site and click Start. It's going on right now. What we do when we begin to worship the Lord is simply join the continual praise that never ceases.

Perhaps the next time you think about a field where you're *not*, but you know some big gobblers are there, appearing to float in the grass at full strut, or you think of a duck blind or deer stand where the mallards, bucks, and does are without you there to see them, you'll remember that in heaven, "day and night they never cease to say, 'Holy, holy, holy, is the Lord God almighty.'" If so, feel free to join in. God would be honored if you do.

Almighty God of Abraham, Isaac, and Jacob, maker of this universe, I join the hosts of heaven who are, right now, singing praise to You. You alone deserve our worship, adoration, and our thanks for Your loving-kindness toward us. Blessed be Your holy name forever and ever. In the name of Jesus, Your eternal Son, I add my amen and amen!

20

A Home Destroyed

Be of sober spirit, be on the alert. Your adversary, the devil, prowls around like a roaring lion, seeking someone to devour.

1 PETER 5:8

When I was about fourteen, a friend and I went squirrel hunting with our twenty-gauge shotguns. After a couple hours of watching and waiting in different areas, neither of us had put a bushy tail in the game pockets of our coats. We met up at the top of the hill and decided to walk down the ridge a couple of hundred yards to another spot. All the while we watched for movement in the branches overhead, listening for any rustling in the dry leaves and the familiar scratchy squawking sound that squirrels make. Finally we caught sight of a lone acorn eater about thirty yards ahead of us, hightailing it up a tall oak.

We watched the gray squirrel rocket to the top of the tree and then disappear into a tightly packed clump of leaves that looked slightly larger than a basketball. The leafy wad was its home.

My friend and I hurried to the base of the towering tree, put our thumbs on the hammer of our guns and quietly waited for the squirrel to reappear. Five minutes or so went by, and impatience got the best of both of us. It was time to act.

It's been too long to remember which of us suggested our next move, but there was no hesitation when the idea came up. We raised our single-shot twenty-gauges toward the nest, took aim, and fired.

As the double load of buckshot ripped through the brown mass, the whole thing seemed to lift and then settle back into the fork of branches that held it. Suddenly two mortally wounded squirrels came tumbling out of the nest, falling limp to the ground near our feet. We were stunned. Another one attempted to escape, but it was not quick enough to outrun our second shots. We bagged it too, then quickly reloaded and waited another half minute to see if a fourth squirrel would appear. Seeing no more movement in the treetop nest, we lowered our shotguns and congratulated each other for taking out three squirrels with only two shots.

While walking back to my friend's house, I didn't feel the least bit regretful about emptying loads of buckshot into the squirrels' residence. But later that night was a different story for me. As I lay on my bed, mentally replaying what we had done, I realized I had taken part in violently and unfairly destroying a nest that was meant to be a safe place for the squirrel family. Reality fell heavy on my heart.

Before I fell asleep I promised myself I would never again shoot into a squirrel's nest—and I haven't. I will admit, however, if those I love were starving, I would do whatever was necessary to provide sustenance for them. Other than that, I wouldn't shoot another nest for the thrill of the kill.

What took place on that West Virginia hilltop all those years ago holds a sobering illustration that's worth noting. The houses where we live are like the squirrel's nest in that they are supposed to be where we can find shelter, safety, rest, and companionship. The hunter (unfortunately me in this case) and his weapon is like the devil who, as 1 Peter

5:8 describes him, goes through the woods seeking whom he may shoot. Satan's mission is to steal, kill, and destroy, and with the blast of his evil gun, he targets entire homes. His shotgun shells are filled with the deadly buckshot of destructive things like greed, envy, depraved entertainment, addiction, jealousy, fear, technological distractions, and doubt. With them he fires into our homes mercilessly, and his goal is compete destruction.

What is the answer to prevent making our homes so vulnerable to the devil? It's illustrated in another type of home that squirrels use, namely, the hollows of trees. If that first squirrel we spotted on the hilltop had run into a hole in the tree instead of his leafy loft, my friend and I would have walked away knowing it was worthless to spray his house with our guns. Hiding behind the protection of the thickness of his hardwood home, the squirrel and his family would have been safe.

That thick-trunked tree is a reminder of the cross of Christ. Made of wood, the cross is where victory over the enemy of our souls was forever accomplished, and it's where my family and I can go for protection against Satan's attempts to annihilate us.

The triumph that the old wooden cross represents is
where I want us to always run when the devil comes
sneaking into our neck of the woods.

O merciful and powerful God,
thank You for the security You provide
us through the triumph of the cross
of Christ. It is the home of our souls
where we know You will always shield
us from the Evil One who wants to
destroy us not only as individuals but
as entire families. I bless Your name for this
provision, and I'm grateful for the peace and rest
we can enjoy by dwelling in Your house. Amen.

21

Closer

I did not come to call the
righteous, but sinners.

MARK 2:17

One word that hunters often use is *closer*. I don't mean *closer* with the *s* sounding like a *z*, as in someone who shuts a door. The word I refer to is the one that hunters whisper when an animal or bird is slowly coming in but holding back, just out of range. It's those moments when the word can turn into a desperate plea with prayer overtones. That's how I meant it during spring gobbler season as I sat at a field edge behind a knee-high blind made of some brush I had gathered from the immediate area.

My intent was to conceal myself from a group of turkeys I thought would show up. There were three huge long beards in the bunch, and my goal was to take one home for Annie to fry for the evening supper we were planning for our entire family.

My crossbow was cocked, resting on my knee, when, just as I predicted, five hens and three mature males entered the field about a hundred yards from me. They started feeding and meandering toward me. All I had to do was wait with the bow on my knee and my trigger finger lightly touching the safety lever.

Like it always does when turkeys very slowly move across a field, they seemed to take a week to cover half the distance between us. The hens pecked at the bugs, but the gobblers didn't take a single bite. All they did was strut and appear to float on the grass, trying to impress the ladies. When the group was about forty-five yards away, their progress in my direction went from slow and steady to really slow.

As I waited, I put my cheek down to the stock of the crossbow so I could see through the peep sight. I placed the neon green dot inside the circle on the kill zone of the bigger gobbler and rehearsed my upcoming shot. I wasn't about to pull the trigger at that distance for a self-imposed reason.

Even though my carbon-fiber bolt travels at an amazingly fast speed—nearly two hundred feet per second—for the sake of a sure shot, I'd rather not shoot at anything farther away than twenty-five to thirty yards. I don't want to risk the target hearing the *thwap* of the collapsing bow limbs and having enough time to move even a little bit before the traveling shaft can hit its mark. So I waited.

A few minutes passed and the birds were about forty-yards out. Feeling a little concerned that the group might change direction or, worse, get busted by something like a stray dog or coyote, I started pleading my case in a repeated whisper.

"Closer…C'mon…closer…"

As if they could hear me, the birds obeyed my command and continued moving toward me.

"Closer…Closer…C'mon…"

Finally, the trio of males followed the hens to within twenty yards of my bow and kept coming. Fifteen…ten…eight yards. Why wait any longer?

Snap! The distinct sound of the sudden collapse of the crossbow limbs sent all the birds flying—except one. The ten-inch gobbler flopped a few times and then went motionless. The deal was done. My prayer-like wish that he would come closer came true.

If you're a hunter, you've whispered the word "closer" a time or two just like I did when I arrowed the gobbler. If you haven't, you will. When it happens, I hope you'll be reminded of the fact that, when it comes to God's desire for sinners, He *wants* them to come near to Him. Second Thessalonians 2:13-14 says, "But we should always give thanks to God for you, brethren beloved by the Lord, because God has chosen you from the beginning for salvation through sanctification by the Spirit and faith in the truth. It was for this *He called you* through our gospel" (emphasis added).

The good news is, unlike my whispered wish for the gobbler to come closer so I could take its life, God whispers to the hearts of sinners, "Closer…C'mon, closer…" to give them life, even life everlasting. The last few words of verse 14 promise "that you may gain the glory of our Lord Jesus Christ."

No one can come to Me unless the Father who sent Me draws him; and I will raise him up on the last day (John 6:44).

Almighty God, I offer You my deepest thanks for wanting me to come closer to You. To think that You, the Maker and God of this entire universe, would long for my presence is a blessing that has value that cannot be measured. Being drawn to You through the Spirit of Christ has blessed my life here on earth beyond measure. You are indeed wonderful. In Your Son's holy name, I say amen.

22

Stone's Throw Away

He who is without sin among you, let him
be the first to throw a stone at her.

JOHN 8:7

I heard a story about a pair of game wardens in
Indiana who waited until well after dark to set up
a fake buck deer in a field along a country road.
Their mission was to catch lawbreakers who used
spotlights for nighttime hunting.

The decoy, nicknamed Timex because it took
a lickin' and kept on tickin', had a remotely con-
trolled motorized head and a really nice trophy
rack. Because the realistic features were very effective at capturing the attention of poachers, the two
wardens had issued three fines before midnight to
passersby who had fired at it. They decided to wait
for one more taker before they headed home.

Sure enough a truck came down the road shining a million-candle spotlight into the field. The wardens watched as the truck came to a stop and the driver got out. He removed a rifle from behind his seat, stepped to the front left fender of the pickup, and laid the gun across the hood. As he took aim the wardens decided to quietly cross the road and confront him. One of them broke the silence with a challenge.

"Nice deer, but I don't think you wanna shoot it."

The night hunter turned and saw the officer's uniform in the residual light of his front beams and pushed the safety button on his rifle back to the on position.

"No sir. You're right. I don't reckon I wanna take the shot."

The officer chose to be lenient and said, "I'm not gonna issue you a ticket tonight since you didn't take a shot, but you came mighty close to doing something that could have cost you a lot of money. Take tonight as a warning not to hunt for deer this way. Its not smart."

The man thanked the game wardens and drove away. I imagine realizing he was one squeeze of a trigger from making a huge mistake stole some sleep from him. If he hadn't heeded the unexpected challenge from the merciful game warden, he would have lost his truck, his gun, his hunting license, and a big wad of cash to the fine he'd have to pay.

The night hunter's close call with major trouble has a familiar biblical ring to it. Based on the John 8 story of the woman caught in the act of adultery, the following song lyric shows the similarity.

Stone's Throw Away

He was in the crowd that day
Had a stone in his hand
To throw it at that woman
It was an evil plan
But Jesus started writing on the ground
And by the time He was through
He had turned the tables
He showed him the cold, hard truth
That he was just a stone's throw away
From making a bad choice
So close to going astray
Until he heard that voice

"You're gonna get off track
You gotta leave and not look back!"
He was just a stone's throw away
From doing something crazy

As it turned out, when the man was confronted with the fact that his sin gave him no right to stone the adulterous woman, he dropped his stone and walked away. It was a smart thing to do.

Here's the second verse of the song lyric. It offers another example of a brush with spiritual disaster.

She was on the bridge that day
Holding her wedding band
Gonna throw it in that river
There was another man
But then she heard the Spirit whisper in her
    heart
"You're on a dead-end road
So put that ring on your finger
It's time to go back home."
She was just a stone's throw away
From making a bad choice
So close to going astray
Until she heard that voice

"You're gonna get off track
You gotta leave and not look back!"
She was just a stone's throw away
From doing something crazy.*

The good news is the wife did indeed heed the warning in her soul to recommit to her marriage. It was not an easy thing to do, and it took some time for her relationship to be strong again. But it was worth it.

Enough about others. How about you?

Are you just a stone's throw away from making a bad choice?

So close to going astray, but do you hear that voice?

"You're gonna get off track. You gotta leave and not look back!"

Are you just a stone's throw away from doing something crazy?

---

* Steve Chapman and Jeff Pearles, Times & Seasons Music, Inc., BMI, Jeffed Music, BMI, 2015.

O merciful Father, You know my heart. The last thing I want to do is ignore the warning You give regarding doing what's right. Help me to choose righteousness over unrighteousness. I need the strength You alone can give to have the courage to walk away from the sin I know would so easily entangle me. I want to do this to Your glory and to that alone. In Christ's name. I ask for Your help. Amen.

23

Who He Is, Who He Was

Honor your father and mother.

EPHESIANS 6:2

"Honor your father and your mother" is the fifth of the Ten Commandments written by the very hand of God (Exodus 20:12). While it was given with no exception clause or footnote that says you can skip to the next commandment if you have horrific parents, it did come with a promise of a long life for those who obey it.

Perhaps the promise of living long on the earth is divine compensation for those who show respect for parents even though they didn't earn it. Another possible reason for the added promise is that God, in His great wisdom, knew that it would be a very good thing for children to live a long time so they could care for their parents when they may need it in their latter years. (The timing of this sounds as if God arranged it, doesn't it?) Such was the case for a father and son whose story is in the following lyric.

Who He Is, Who He Was

I sat in that hospital room
Where I'd been with Dad so many times
And wondered how many memories
Had been stolen from his mind
He seemed so lost and so confused
Not even sure why I came
I was another stranger to him
Even though our names are the same
But I knew one thing is true...
Who he is and who he was
They both deserve my love
He took care of me back then
I'll be here right now for him
I know he needs me and I'll do it because
Of who he is and who he was

I thought about when I was a boy
He could lift me over his head
He played catch every Saturday
And he prayed beside my bed

Sometimes he had to work two jobs
Just to try to make ends meet
My dad was a superman no one could ever
    beat
And you can bet I won't forget
Who he is and who he was
They both deserve my love
He took care of me back then
I'll be here right now for him
I know he needs me and I'll do it because
Of who he is and who he was

And one of these days
He's gonna be made whole
And it's all because God knows
Who he is and who he was.*

Obviously, the key to this dad being honored by
his son in such a beautiful and significant way was
that the dad had previously earned his son's respect.
Perhaps this touching story will encourage we who
are parents to seriously consider how we are treating our children. May we not forget that the key to
being honored as a parent is to parent honorably.

---

* Steve Chapman, Times & Seasons Music Inc., BMI, Tim Morgan,
Mathis Mountain Music, LLC, 2014.

Father in heaven, help me live in such a way before my children that they won't find it difficult to obey Your command to honor me as their parent. Thank You in advance for any benefit I may reap in my late years from treating my children in a godly way as they are growing up. And as a child, I thank You for the blessing of a long life that comes with showing respect for my father and mother. I want to always honor them even in the face of their failures, because I know that, ultimately, You are honored by it. In Christ's name, amen.

24

Eat the Scroll

Then He said to me, "Son of man,
eat what you find; eat this scroll, and
go, speak to the house of Israel."

EZEKIEL 3:1

God's instruction in Ezekiel 3:1 for the prophet to "eat this scroll, and go, speak to the house of Israel" sounds very strange. I can't help but imagine a man tearing off pieces of paper and eating them. Of course, God was directing the prophet to "take into your heart all My words which I will speak to you and listen closely. Go to the exiles, to the sons of your people, and speak to them and tell them, whether they listen or not. 'Thus says the Lord GOD'" (verses 10-11).

There were three commands Ezekiel was to obey:

1. Consume God's words and make them a part of his entire inner being.

2. Listen closely for God to tell him what to say with the word that he had eaten, who to say it to, and when to say it.

3. To be bold enough to say what he was told to say whether the intended hearer listened or not.

Ezekiel's calling required an approach that would not qualify today as politically correct. Yet I'm sure if he were here today, it would not stop him from being obedient to God's command to speak the truth to whoever he was told to say it. Why? Because there were consequences if he didn't follow God's order. It's mentioned in verses 16-18.

At the end of seven days the word of the LORD came to me, saying, "Son of man, I have appointed you a watchman to the house of Israel; whenever you hear a word from My mouth, warn them from Me. When I say to the wicked, 'You will surely die,' and you do not warn him or speak out to warn the wicked from his wicked way that he may live, that wicked man shall die in his iniquity, but his blood I will require at your hand."

Then in verse 20, God goes a little further and includes some instruction regarding the righteous.

Again, when a righteous man turns away from his righteousness and commits iniquity, and I place an obstacle before him, he will die; since you have not warned him, he shall die in his sin, and his righteous deeds which he has done shall not be remembered; but his blood I will require at your hand.

I can see why Ezekiel would be obedient to warn whomever he was told to warn. Being responsible for someone's demise due to not alerting them about their sin would be plenty of motivation to obey the Lord's urging to extend the warning. Plus, if he did obey the command to speak up and the warning was ignored, he was released from the responsibility for their destruction. That, too, would behoove Ezekiel to obey.

What about those today who are not prophets and do not hear God speak to us like He spoke to Ezekiel? Are we to be as bold as he was to warn someone who is sinning that their unrighteous choices will lead to their destruction? If so, are the consequences the same if we fail to warn them? The best answer I can give is found in James 5:19-20.

> My brethren, if any among you strays from the truth and one turns him back, let him know that he who turns a sinner from the error of his way will save his soul from death and will cover a multitude of sins.

It seems that this verse is more than a mere suggestion. It's a timeless, God-initiated directive to all of us who belong to God's family to be caring enough to warn anyone, saint and sinner, to turn from their error. The question is, have we eaten the scroll of God's Word so that it is such a part of our being that we know what to say on His behalf?

If your answer is "no," then it's time to start eating! If your answer is "yes," then the next question is, Will you be bold enough to discretely warn someone about the danger of their waywardness when the opportunity comes? If not, keep in mind that their salvation is at risk. Whether it concerns your family member, a friend, a coworker, or a fellow believer, don't forget that "he who turns a sinner from the error of his way will save his soul from death and will cover a multitude of sins." What greater reward could there be for your boldness?

God, thank You for feeding my soul with the scroll of Your Word. I know it will prepare me well if I'm to speak on Your behalf. I realize that approaching someone about their sin can be as risky today as it was in Ezekiel's day, but I don't want to fail to follow Your urging to do so. I must confess that the possibility of being called hateful, intolerant, nosy, or an extremist is troubling, but help me not focus on the negative result of warning someone about sin but on the positive. When I feel hesitant to speak for You, help me to do so with a humble attitude that comes from having experienced Your tender grace and mercy and to speak boldly because of the authority of Your written Word, which

I have consumed. I need these qualifications if I am to confidently warn sinners as well as Your followers who have strayed from You that their error will destroy them. I know that to do so is an act of kindness that can save their souls from everlasting death and separation from You. I want to know the joy of that outcome more than I want to be politically, socially, or culturally correct. I pray this prayer in the mighty name of Your loving Son, Jesus. Amen.

25

Remember Me

He was saying, "Jesus, remember me
when You come in Your kingdom!"

LUKE 23:42

If you are a deer hunter who favors tree-stand hunting and you're familiar with the Scriptures that describe the crucifixion of Jesus, I have a question for you. Have you ever been in a stand and looked to your right or left and imagined seeing Jesus hanging next to you on a tree? I can tell you it's a sobering thought that generates some very strong feelings.

I realize that putting myself in the place of one of the thieves who hung next to Christ sounds odd, but I was moved by the imagery of it. Of course, I wouldn't want to have been the criminal who verbally abused Jesus by sarcastically saying, "Are You not the Christ? Save Yourself and us!" (Luke 23:39).

Instead, I would prefer to have been the thief who managed to endear himself to the dying Savior by challenging the other thief's insults when he said, "Do you not even fear God, since you are under the same sentence of condemnation? And we indeed are suffering justly, for we are receiving what we deserve for our deeds; but this man has done nothing wrong" (verse 41).

The next words from the humbled thief were apparently repeated more than once, because verse 42 starts with the phrase "And he was saying." Facing a sure death, it's no wonder the man would repeat, "Jesus, remember me when You come in Your kingdom." He surely wanted to make certain that his desperate request was heard.

The thief's repentance was indeed heard and honored. What an incredible depth of relief the man must have felt when Jesus responded, "Truly I say to you, today you shall be with Me in Paradise" (verse 43).

The blessed reality is that any sinner who realizes they are spiritually lost and in need of redemption can borrow the thief's words said to Jesus and they will not be ignored. That's good news indeed.

Remember Me

O Lord, I know that I'm not worthy
To receive Your mercy
Yet You look at me
With eyes full of love and pity
Please forgive me
As you have done
For those
Who watch us die
In this hour
Hear my cry
Lord will You remember?
Will You remember?
When this life is over
Remember me
There's nothing
I can offer
For Your favor
O Savior
When You come
Into Your kingdom
Remember…me
I am lost, I know it's true
But my hope is now in You.*

---

* Steve Chapman, Times & Seasons Music, Inc., BMI, 2013.

26

Look Up

When these things begin to come to
pass, then look up, and lift up your heads;
for your redemption draweth nigh.

LUKE 21:28 KJV

It's hard to tell how many of us modern, electronic-device-carrying hunters have missed a lifetime shot because we were focusing on the face of a phone when a trophy appeared. It makes me wonder how many camo-cased phones have been thrown over a cliff or into a river because the hunter realized what had happened.

Most of us are aware that as useful as a cell phone can be, it is one of the greatest hindrances to good old eye-to-eye communication. Not only that, being distracted by a phone can be deadly, like it was for the woman in a bustling Northeast city who was apparently texting when she stepped off the curb and into the path of a bus she didn't see coming. It was her last text.

Another phenomena that develops with phones are the neck and back disorders in people who use technology excessively. These skeletal and muscular problems affect all ages, but it's especially worse in younger people who spend hours every day on social media sites.

With the goal of reminding anyone who will listen, including my family and friends, the following song lyric was written as a call to look up! To help me say it as clearly as possible, I enlisted the help of two songwriting buddies who also feel frustrated that the device disease has so profoundly afflicted our world.

Look Up

How I long to see your face
It would make my day to see your smile
But you've been captured by that screen
For a while
If you would take a little break
And let me see what's in your eyes
I want to know your hopes and dreams

I just want a minute of your time
Look up! Hey, look up!
There's so much you're missing
That makes life worth living
Looking down, you just won't see enough
Look up!

We're not sure tomorrow's gonna come
Right now is all we have, it's true
So can we turn off everything
So I could have a heart to heart with you
Look up! Hey, look up!*

There's at least one other interesting possibility I've thought about regarding our technical divisives, er, devices. I wonder if God, in His ability to see into the future, prompted Luke to address the global distraction that our eye-occupying phones, pads, smart watches, and so on would become in the last days. It could be why he wrote, "When these things begin to come to pass, then look up, and lift up your heads; for your redemption draweth nigh" (Luke 21:28).

---

* Steve Chapman, Lindsey Williams, and Tim Morgan, Times & Seasons Music, BMI, Really Big Bison Music, SESAC, Mathis Mountain Music (LLC), 2015.

Of course, the warning to look up may not be a direct reference to our handhelds, but at least it's interesting to explore the connection, especially at this time in history when technology consumes so much of our attention. With this in mind, let's unpack the idea a little more.

Luke 21:25-28 includes a long list of things that will happen prior to Christ's coming. He writes of nations rising against nations, earthquakes, wars, famines, pestilences, and fearful sights in the heavens. Luke then calls for God followers to give a two-step reaction to seeing the culmination of the signs: look up and lift up your heads.

The phrase "look up" literally means to "straighten up." In other words, come out of your humped-over position, sit up straight, and look around. While it is likely a command that is directed to those whose backs are bent under the weight of worry over impending doom, couldn't the words of the verse be just as applicable to the average smartphone user these days?

If you've recently been in an airport gate area, a hospital waiting room, at a ball game, and even at a family reunion and observed the folks around you, you know what I mean. So many of them have their head down with their back painfully rounded as they sit, absorbed by their device.

Unfortunately, it takes a real jolt for some people to straighten their backs. In an airport, for example, just about everyone will look up when someone trips the alarm on a security door. The loud, ear-piercing siren doesn't go unnoticed when it sounds. People shift in their chairs, sit up, and look around with concern for their safety.

Spiritually, to get people to look up, it seems that a similarly powerful jolt is needed. Could it be that the list of dreadful things that will take place prior to our redemption is that biblical blast that will prompt people to straighten up and look around?

Why is it important to first look up? On a physical level, when one straightens their back, physiologically it's easier to lift their heads. Spiritually, when we see the signs of the times coming to pass and respond to them by deliberately straightening up and giving God our attention, then we can more easily lift our eyes to the heavens. God has invited us to do this because He doesn't want us to miss the amazing thing that is going to happen. We will see "the Son of Man coming in a cloud with power and great glory" (verse 27).

I certainly don't want to be all humped over and looking down when that happens. Surely you don't want that either. Let's look up!

God, right now the signs of Your coming that were written about in Luke are happening in our world. I don't want to be so immersed in the endless and often needless conversations and entertainment my handheld device offers that I would be spiritually slumped over and inattentive. Help me to be one who is looking up so I can turn my eyes to the sky and see Your glorious appearance in the heavens. I pray this for myself, my loved ones, and my friends as well. God help us all to look up! In the name of the coming Lord Jesus Christ, amen.

27

The Assistant Guide

I have no one else of kindred spirit.

<small>PHILIPPIANS 2:20</small>

One of my most memorable hunting trips was in the area of Sitka, Alaska, to hunt the mighty brown bear. On day two of a ten-day hunt, Dale Adams (owner of Adams Alaskan Safaris) put me on to a massive brownie. Facing a nine footer that lumbered down the beach toward us was a heart-pounding, soul-searching string of minutes. It took three pulls of my trigger to stop the thick-haired beast—and a shot for good measure from my safety-conscious guide.

With the unforgettable encounter happening early in the trip, releasing the pressure valve, I had lots of time to relax and enjoy the countless nearby islands as we sailed on a boat named *Surveyor*. During the evenings Dale departed with another hunter, leaving me and my Tennessee friend and videographer Lindsey Williams in the capable hands of his assistant guide, Alex Carter.

During some adventures that included accompanying Alex on a few bear scouting and fishing trips, Lindsey and I enjoyed learning more about the young Arkansas native who was the right-hand man to a legendary Alaskan guide.

Knowing that we were a couple of Tennessee songwriters and hearing a sample of our lyrics while visiting in the pilothouse of the *Surveyor* one evening, Alex decided he'd try his hand at poetically describing his role. He disappeared below decks and then reappeared with a sheet of yellow notebook paper with writing on both sides. He read the following to us:

The Assistant Guide

It's April and time to get on the *Surveyor*
I weigh 165 pounds, barely made it through
    the winter,
And my wallet needs to gain some weight too
I fly off like a soldier headed to battle
And catch the milk run north from Seattle,

Tires touch down at Sitka at 11 p.m.

"Welcome to Hades," Dale says to me at the
airport,

Not sure if that's the hunting or the weather
report,

Doesn't matter, we're underway tomorrow at
seven

The clients arrive and are all gung-ho,

So ready or not, here we go,

Skiffs are launched and the guns are sighted
in

We motor away so full I could die,

Why did I have two pieces of peanut butter
pie?

Lori's trying to kill me with a spoon!

The wind is blowing near gale; I'm fighting
for stability

And the hunter has a childlike faith in my
ability

To steer the boat to the bear of his dreams

Now if I don't kill a bear by at least day two

Adams will tag out, and my hunt will be
through

Have to try again after the next turnaround

After spotting a few dinks and a sow

I see one I want to be on the beach with now
The tide is coming up, but the sun is going
     down
After a forty-five-minute long stalk
Somehow we managed to not click a rock
And we're seventy-five yards away
The wind is blowing steady out of the west
And my hunter has a solid rest…and I realize
Very soon I'll either be a hero or a zero.*

The last line of Alex's poem revealed a mountain of emotion. He was very aware that if his hunter scored and the bear was a bruiser male like he thought it was when he glassed it, he'd be loved and maybe even hugged. But if the shooter failed to close the deal, even if it was his fault, Alex was aware he might get the blame. As painful as that outcome would be, he took comfort in knowing that at least his boss and mentor would appreciate his work, no matter what happened. It was true because there was never any doubt that Alex's main goal was the success of the hunter.

The obvious trust that Dale Adams had for his assistant is pictured in the writings of the apostle Paul and his reference to young Timothy in

---

* Alex Carter, 2015. Used by permission.

Philippians 2:19-23 (NIV): "I hope in the Lord Jesus to send Timothy to you soon, that I also may be cheered when I receive news about you. I have no one else like him, who will show genuine concern for your welfare. For everyone looks out for their own interests, not those of Jesus Christ. But you know that Timothy has proved himself, because as a son with his father he has served with me in the work of the gospel. I hope, therefore, to send him as soon as I see how things go with me."

Taking a cue from the immense value Paul placed on Timothy's assistance, as well as Dale Adams's appreciation of Alex's service, I want to be found as pleasing to God in my role as His assistant in the work of sharing the good news. May it be true for you as well.

Thank You, Lord, that You have entrusted me with the message of hope found in Your saving grace. I want to be found faithful as one of Your assistant guides. May it be so in Your precious and holy name, amen.

28

Eyes Fixed

Fixing our eyes on Jesus.

HEBREWS 12:2

If anyone knows what it means to fix our eyes on something, it's a hunter who has spent a lot of time in the chase. Being one myself, I think it's safe to say that most of us have had times when we've scanned the woods and noticed something slightly different that caught our attention. When that happens, our momentary glance becomes an extended stare.

If we're hunting deer or elk, for example, maybe it's a speck of brown among the foliage that doesn't match anything around it. Perhaps it's a flick of white or a shape that wasn't there before. If our hunt is for a springtime gobbler, our focus might be on an unusually dark spot against a far hillside or a hint of red that seems a little brighter than the other colorful growth.

Without batting an eyelid, we key in on the suspicious sight, taking whatever time is required to find out what it is. How satisfying we feel when that spot of color or that odd shape we've watched for several minutes suddenly moves. At that moment we prove that the combination of patience and fixed eyes is a powerfully effective hunting technique.

There's yet another reason we fix our eyes on a specific, subtle spot when we're hunting. It's because we *want* to see something. It's why we get up at such ridiculously early hours and endure the harshest of nature's challenges, such as bitter cold, driving rain, or gnawing gnats. Seeing game is the name of the game, and aligning our will to the quest is something we understand.

Fixing our eyes on Jesus calls us to do what we do when we hunt, that is, we wake up with the quest on our mind, we set our face toward the place where we'll take our stand, and once there, our greatest hope is to see the slightest evidence of the animal or bird we're there to find.

As followers of Christ, we'll know we have our eyes fixed on Him when we wake up thinking about Him and when we go into the woods of everyday life *wanting* to see evidence of His presence in our family, our friendships, our work, our leisure, and our society.

Do we long to see Him? If we do, there is a benefit to be enjoyed. It's explained in Hebrews 12:2-3:

> Fixing our eyes on Jesus the author and perfecter of faith, who for the joy set before Him endured the cross, despising the shame, and has sat down at the right hand of the throne of God. For consider Him who has endured such hostility by sinners against Himself, so that you will not grow weary and lose heart.

When we live with a determination to keep our eyes on the Lord, He will see to it that our faith will be made stronger and our weariness of heart will be replaced with spiritual vigor. I want that for me, and I'm sure you want it for yourself as well.

Father in heaven, thank You for the eyes to see the signs of Your presence in this life. I pray for Your strength and grace to help me to always want to see You and to help me look past the distractions of emotions like worry, fear, doubt, or anything else that would take my focus off of You. I bless Your name for making Yourself visible to me through faith, and I set my will to keep my eyes fixed on You and Your goodness. In Your Son's name I pray, amen.

29

Amazed but Not Surprised

When Peter saw this, he said to them: "Fellow
Israelites, why does this surprise you?"

ACTS 3:12 NIV

During our Tennessee spring gobbler season I
enjoy getting texts from my friend Jason Cruise.
When I see his name on my phone screen, I know
I'm going to see a photo of him smiling behind the
fan of another huge turkey-dactil. The messages he
includes are always fun. He might say, "Took two
hours to pull him in" or "I introduced Mr. Big Bird
to Mr. Mossberg!"

When I respond to Jason's reports about his turkey hunts, I never say anything like "I'm totally
surprised you could get that old gobbler to com-
mit to your call." To make such a statement would

be a veiled insult. It would mean I had my doubts he knew enough about how to outsmart an old gobbler with his mouth or slate call to get the job done.

Instead, I usually answer with a short and sweet "Awesome, dude" or "You're amazing" or "Not a jealous bone in my body!" What I want Jason to know is that I think he's the best turkey hunter who ever put on camo, and there's not a bird on the planet that's safe when he's in their neck of the woods. The bottom line is this: I'm not surprised—I'm just amazed.

This reaction seems to have been what the apostle Peter was hoping to draw from the people who witnessed the healing of the lame man as told in Acts 3. After saying those notable words, "I do not possess silver and gold, but what I do have I give to you" (verse 6), and lifting the man to his feet, the people standing nearby and seeing the miracle were totally shocked.

Seeing all their stunned expressions, Peter said, "Why are you surprised? Is it because you thought we could do this in our own power? No, no! The

God of Abraham, Isaac, and Jacob, the God of our fathers, has glorified His servant Jesus, the one you disowned and wanted killed.…It is the name of Jesus that has strengthened this man who you see and know…and the faith that comes through Him has given this lame man perfect health in the presence of you all" (my paraphrase of verses 11-16).

In so many words, Peter challenged the crowd to understand that to be so surprised by what they had seen revealed their lack of faith in God. Their response was a response of doubt. Instead, he said, to be amazed by the miracle was to reveal confidence that God was able to heal anyone. They should have responded with praise.

Maybe you'll remember this story the next time you hear God has done something remarkable in your life. Perhaps a physical or emotional healing in you or a family member, a personal need miraculously met, or a friend you've been praying for a long time would make a wise decision actually does so. If so, don't be so surprised by God's great ability. Instead, give Him the praise He's due by simply saying to Him, "You're amazing!"

Blessed God and Father of Abraham, Isaac, and Jacob, You are indeed *amazing*. I use the word with all the praise for You I can muster in my spirit. I want to always be amazed by You, and never do I want to imply in any way that I doubt Your might.
To Your glory I pray in Christ's name, amen.

30

Believe It to See It

Jesus said to him, "Because you have
seen Me, have you believed? Blessed are
they who did not see, and yet believed."

JOHN 20:29

Several years ago I set aside some time and forked
over some hard-earned cash to make a trip to one
of the Dakotas. I did it for one good reason. A man
who owned a huge farm there came to me after my
wife and I staged a concert in that area. He told me
he had seen mule deer bucks in the territory that
appeared to be in the three-hundred-pound range.
He invited me to come hunt.

I was sure he saw my eyebrows raise and my eyes
widen when I heard him say three hundred. Hoping he didn't detect the doubt I had in what he said,
I continued to listen as he told me about the area

in which he lived. The more he talked, the stronger my curiosity grew.

By the time our conversation ended, I was ready to pack my bags and head his way. He didn't show me a picture to prove his claim or give me a phone number of someone I could call to validate it. I didn't need it. I was hooked and I planned to see him again.

When October came that year, I found myself trekking up and down the hills of northern South Dakota with my .270 rifle. I won't forget the awe I felt when I looked into a ravine and saw a manifestation of the farmer's claim. It took two shots at a little over one hundred yards to close the deal.

Weighing in at nearly 290 pounds, the four-by-four mule buck was and still is the biggest deer I have ever taken. His head mount is at my house, and it evokes great memories every time I look at it. I'm so grateful for the gentleman's invitation to hunt on his property, and I'm equally glad I didn't discount his report about the deer that roamed his land.

There's something else that makes me think of that South Dakota hunt. Two friends and I were writing a song together and chasing an idea based on John 20:29. Jesus is talking to the disciple called Doubting Thomas: "Blessed are they who did not see, and yet believed." I realized that my believing the farmer's claim before I saw proof of it is a pretty good illustration of those of us who believe in Christ even though we're yet to see Him.

Here are the lyrics we wrote. I think you'll get the connection.

Believe It to See It

It was a Sunday morning Mary came runnin'
With news that just wouldn't keep
Said the stone at the Jesus grave has been
    rolled away
And the angel said to me
He's risen from the dead just like He said
And soon you'll see him face to face
But Thomas had his doubts what the girl was
    talkin' 'bout
You could say he had a question of faith
You gotta believe it to see it
You gotta take Him at His word
Trust and you can stand upon every promise
That you've ever heard

Oh blessed are those who have not seen
But say "amen" to every word in red
'Cause if Jesus said it, so be it
You gotta believe it to see it.
If we were being honest, we've been like
        Thomas
Tempted with a doubt or two
But you can turn the situation into an
        occasion
For a heavenly point of view
Oh this could prove to be an opportunity
For the Lord to show
He's your confidence no matter what the
        circumstance
If you want your faith to grow
You gotta believe it to see it
You gotta take Him at His word
Trust and you can stand upon every promise
That you've ever heard
Oh blessed are those who have not seen
But say amen to every word in red
'Cause if Jesus said it, so be it
You gotta believe it to see it.*

---

*   S. Chapman, Lindsey Williams, and Kenna Turner West, Times &
Seasons Music, Inc., BMI, Really Big Bison Productions, SESAC, Daywind Music, BMI 2013. Used by permission.

Lord of all truth, I say thanks to You for sending Your Holy Spirit to speak to my heart about Your majesty and grace as well as the salvation You provided through Your sacrifice. I am yet to see You, but I believe You are who You say You are. Blessed be Your holy name. In Christ I pray, amen.

31

Backyard Hunter

Therefore, get rid of all moral filth and the evil
that is so prevalent and humbly accept the
word planted in you, which can save you.

JAMES 1:21 NIV

Summertime is a tough time for many hunters—
at least for the law-abiding kind. Because seasons
are closed for deer, turkey, squirrel, rabbit, duck,
and all the other big and small game that we chase,
we're left to twiddle our hammer-cocking thumbs
and wait. But not me. I'm a summer hunter.

Many mornings I get up and head to my back
porch, take the pair of shovels leaning against the
wall, and hunt one of the most illusive creatures
God ever made: moles.

The tactic that has yielded the most success for
me is to softly step to within a few yards of where
a tunnel exists and keep an eye on it. I monitor the

very end of the tunnel and watch for any telltale upheaval of dirt and grass. It's a very subtle movement and therefore hard to detect, but if I see it I know that right beneath the surface of the ground is the little bane of my backyard.

It's tempting to break into a dead run toward a spot that just moved, but I know the best thing to do is to let the furry burrower work forward a few more inches, just to make sure I'm not imagining the lift of the soil. If the detection is confirmed, then I pounce.

To avoid alerting the critter that I'm stalking, I tip-toe to the scene of the crime in progress and carefully lay one of the shovels on the ground but keep it within reach. I thrust the other shovel blade perpendicular to the tunnel line, about two feet from the end. Now I have a block to thwart any attempt at escape. Then I pick up my other shovel and jab it into the ground as deep as I can, just beside the end of the tunnel. With one fluid motion I pop the shovel full of dirt into the air. More times than not, a dark-colored, paddle-footed, no-eyed, sharp-nosed enemy flies heavenward for a moment before falling back to earth, where he or she (it doesn't matter to me) meets a quick demise.

I can't sufficiently describe the joy and satisfaction I feel when I eliminate a yard wrecker. Of course my joy comes at the expense of the mole and the momentary pain it encounters. Okay, I admit that maybe, for a few seconds, I feel a little sorrow for the tiny guy or gal. They're so furry and soft, and they appear so amazingly clean, considering where they live. But before I can sigh in sadness, I look around the yard and see the network of damage the moles have done, and all the gloom goes away.

One day while reading the book of James, one of the verses reminded me of my mole quest: "Therefore, get rid of all moral filth and the evil that is so prevalent" (1:21 NIV). I did a quick study on the verse and learned that the picture in the original writing used for "get rid of" is that of taking off dirty clothes. If I had written that verse today, I might have used the image of ridding my yard of destructive moles. My intent is the same; that is, to help the saints know that filth and evil can do great damage to one's life. For that reason the moles of filth and evil need to be pinpointed and eliminated.

To do so requires our understanding of what they are.

The word *filth* comes from the word *rhuparia*, which refers to moral defilement or impurity. In addition, the word is also connected to a term used for earwax buildup. Getting rid of moral filth (such as sexual perversion and debauchery) results in being better able to hear God's guidance through His written Word.

Evil is from the original word *kakia*. It refers to an intentional corruption that secretly resides in the heart, like a mole that roams my yard, out of sight but just below the surface. Sins like greed, envy, jealousy, and addiction to pornography are some of the concealed evils that destroy a soul.

Once these moles are located, getting rid of them through repentance is desperately needed. When we confess our sins, we eliminate the things that keep us from hearing and understanding God's Word as well as ridding ourselves of the things that do damage to our lives.

Do you have any moles in the yard of your life? If so, may God help you today as you take up your shovels of confession and repentance and go hunting!

Father in heaven, thank You for loving me even though my life has been damaged by sin. Help me identify the things that do not please You, and grant me courage to do what is necessary to get rid of them. Forgive me for letting them damage me for so long. I need Your grace to be healed and whole. In Christ's name, amen.

32

Will To, Want To

On the glorious splendor of Your majesty
And on Your wonderful works, I will meditate.

PSALM 145:5

If you looked up the work "scatterbrained" in a dictionary, you'd probably find a snapshot of my mind. At any given moment I can be thinking about a line in a song lyric that's got me stumped, what's next on my to-do list, an email that needs a reply, where should I set up a deer stand or a question like, "Where did I put my keys?"

While I'm grateful to have a very active mind, it presents a challenge when it comes to one of the most important things I can do to strengthen my relationship with God. I find it very difficult to meditate for very long on His written Word and His amazing attributes. Every time I read the verses that encourage meditating, I feel guilty that I fail at it so often. Yet I know I have to keep trying.

One thing that helps me to not give up in my quest to be better at meditating is to do something I noticed David did in Psalm 145:5: "On the glorious splendor of Your majesty and on Your wonderful works, I *will* meditate" (emphasis added). I don't know if the psalmist meant to imply he had to be deliberate with meditation, but it's the implication I got from it. If David realized he had an overactive mind and he had to rein it in so he could focus on God's attributes, I know how he felt. For me, meditation requires determination. I candidly admit I have to make myself do it.

As hard as it can be for me, I'm encouraged by where David apparently did so much of his thinking on God's greatness. His use of words like "glorious splendor" and "majesty" in Psalm 145 are references to nature. The outdoors seemed to be his favored meditation spot since he mentioned it more than once. For example, Psalm 8:3: "When I consider Your heavens, the work of Your fingers, the moon and the stars, which You have ordained."

Perhaps being in God's great cathedral of the

outdoors was where David found it easier to intentionally focus on his Creator. If so, it could be because being surrounded by God's glorious outdoors is where his "I will meditate" became his "I want to meditate." It's certainly true for me, and the place it happens most often for me is in a deer stand, because it's where:

- There's sustained quiet
- Moving around is restricted
- I'm nowhere near an office, a computer, or a "gotta get it done today" list
- I can't hear the ding or feel the buzz of my phone's text or email alert
- Reading the Word can be done slowly and purposefully

Have you found a special place where it's more conducive for you to focus for a while on God's glory and to contemplate on the guidance He offers in His Word? If not, I'm certain David would recommend the outdoors to you. I certainly do too. I realize that some people can't take advantage of nature's sanctuary due to situations that confine them to the indoors, but if you're able at all, why not give the outdoors a try? Perhaps you'll discover that it's where your "I will meditate" will become your "I want to meditate."

Oh God, our great and awesome Creator, thank You for the beauty of Your earth and the vastness of the sky above it. What a wonderful place to be to see Your greatness and dwell for a while on Your majesty. I trust that when I set my will to go outdoors to enjoy Your presence, You will meet me there. May it be so for the sake of learning even more about who You are. I ask this in Christ's name, amen.

33

Delayed Boom

He said to me, "Do not be afraid, Daniel, for
from the first day that you set your heart on
understanding this and on humbling yourself
before your God, your words were heard, and
I have come in response to your words."

DANIEL 10:12

The first day of muzzleloader season for whitetail finally arrived, and with it came a weather forecast that called for rain. Their predictions were right, but I didn't mind.

As I drove through the predawn darkness toward the Cheatham County farm, I thought of how soft the leaves would be under my boots. It would allow me to do a type of hunting I totally enjoy, namely, stalking quietly and slowly through the woods.

I was so excited about the advantage the rain-drenched forest floor provided, I forgot to consider the negative effect that heavy moisture can have on traditional firearms. I didn't realize it until a sizable six-point buck appeared about fifty yards in front of me, walking from right to left. I was leaning against a tree when I saw him, which gave me a steady rest to use.

When the deer stopped momentarily, I seized the opportunity to take aim. The white, round bead on the front open sights settled into the V of my rear sight and on the lung area of the buck that stood broadside before me. As I put pressure on the trigger, I was sure my willingness to endure the drizzle was about to be rewarded. Then everything went wrong.

When the hammer dropped on the cap, all I heard was a muted pop. It sounded like the noise that the red paper bullet roll made in the toy six-shooter I had when I was a kid. Whether some raindrops had come down the barrel, carrying moisture to the powder, or whether the wetness in the atmosphere had found its way to the charge by another way, I didn't know. What I did know, however, was I had experienced equipment failure.

In that fleeting moment, realizing my cap had

fired but the powder had not ignited, I deliberately fought against the instinct to drop the gun from my shoulder. It's a natural reaction I was taught to avoid, unless, of course, I wanted to risk being sucker punched really hard in the chest or maybe in my teeth by the hard butt of a muzzleloader that could still discharge.

Not wanting to be added to the list of those who have discovered that slow-burning black powder can turn the backside of .50 caliber into the fist of heavyweight boxer, I instantly pressed the stock against my shoulder, kept my aim on the buck, and waited. After about two seconds there was an explosion. The woods filled with smoke and the deal was done.

For a moment I thought I was going to go home with only a breech full of soggy black powder. Instead, I loaded a nice deer in my truck and headed to the processor. I also carried a helpful insight out of the woods that day. Specifically, when a trigger is pulled and nothing happens, it doesn't mean it won't. There could very well be enough fire from the explosion of the cap to start the powder burning and eventually create enough fire in the charge to complete the explosion. Because it might take a few seconds, it's always wise to wait and see.

In a similar way, when we pull the trigger of prayer and ask God for something, we may not get an immediate answer. Sometimes it takes a while. The best biblical illustration for this is noted in the scripture featured with this chapter. Daniel prayed for twenty-one days before he heard an answer boom from heaven.

Sometimes it might take longer for the answer to come. My grandmother Chapman, for example, prayed for the salvation of one of her sons, and he was seventy-four years old before she heard God's report: "Your boy has come home to Me."

Perhaps you have prayed earnestly and in faith about or for something, and you're wondering why you've heard no answer. If so, keep the weapon of prayer to your shoulder—and wait. The response to your words is on its way!

Dear God, You know there are times when I wonder if You hear my prayers. And You know very well I struggle to keep trusting when I'm waiting on Your response. Forgive me for the doubt I've entertained in those times, and grant me the strength to always wait patiently for the answer You will give. In Your Son's name I pray, amen.

34

Faded Label

I prefer black cotton T-shirts not only for everyday wear but when I go hunting. If it's warmer
weather, such as spring gobbler season or early
archery deer season, the material is not only cool,
the darker color doesn't stand out like white cotton
would if any portion of it is seen by the keen eyes
of an animal or bird. While I opt for black T-shirts,
there's one thing about a recently purchased version I don't like. My complaint may sound petty
to some, but to me it's an ongoing source of frus-
tration.

The manufacturers used to sew a tag into the
neckline, but now they've gone tagless. I assume

their intent is to save money and resources but the ink-only-label creates a problem. It starts out bright and visible, but it fades drastically after just a few washes. Consequently, if I get dressed in low light and can't see the print, it's a total guess whether I'll get it right. I can't number the times I've mumbled while removing a shirt to flip it around. (Okay, I know there are a lot of problems in the world that are a lot worse than a backward T-shirt, but I have a feeling I'm not alone in my grumbling.)

As annoying as the tagless tussle can be, at least one good thing has come from it. While getting ready for a midday turkey hunt, I decided, instead of guessing at getting my shirt on right, I'd walk to a window where some light was coming through. I still had to look closely, but finally I saw a hint of the print. In that moment I realized I was looking at a very good illustration of a new convert whose heart was stamped with the name "Christian," but over time their label grew dim.

The reasons are varied when it comes to why the evidence of a person's relationship with Christ may fade. They include a lack of good biblical instruction that can strengthen their resolve to be a faithful follower, the mounting weight of discouragement due to frequent failures, a growing struggle to believe they're truly forgiven for a past sin, or, as 1 Timothy 4:1 mentions, being led astray by deceptive teaching.

The question is, "If you are a disciple of Christ, how readable is the label on your life?"

Has it faded to the point that it's hard to tell if you're on one side or the other? If so, prayerfully read the psalm below and let it become your hope. By the way, if in the future you put on a T-shirt and notice it has a faded label, may it remind you that God alone can brighten the imprint of His grace stamped on your life.

> I waited patiently for the LORD;
> And He inclined to me and heard my cry.
> He brought me up out of the pit of destruction, out of the miry clay,
> And He set my feet upon a rock making my footsteps firm.
> He put a new song in my mouth, a song of praise to our God;
> Many will see and fear
> And will trust in the LORD (Psalm 40:1-3).

35

He Never Misses

So will My word be which goes
forth from My mouth;
It will not return to Me empty,
Without accomplishing what I desire,
And without succeeding in the
matter for which I sent it.

ISAIAH 55:11

There's a beautifully painted wooden sign that stands year round along a local country highway I often travel. It's placed next to a huge pair of open fields that are planted each summer with grains that are specifically favored by birds. The large words on the sign say "Dove Season Opens on Labor Day." Its a never-changing advertisement for hunters to make plans to register, pay the fee, and gather around the massive fields to try their skills at getting the limit of birds for their skillet.

Seeing the advertisement especially around June and July each year stirs me up because by then my longing to hunt has greatly intensified by the months that have passed since spring gobbler season closed. But as exciting as the reminder on the sign is, I know if I take them up on the opportunity to join the other hunters in the field on the first day of dove season, I'll likely not be all that successful in bagging my share of birds. To put it mildly, if it's flying, it's safe around my gun.

I think I have a couple of good excuses for being a poor shot at birds. Being wrong eye dominant for a right-hand shooter makes it tough for me to quickly find and focus on a target. Worse yet, when the target is moving at the relative speed of a bullet, the return on my investment in several pricey boxes of number-seven shells is going to be pitiful at best. All I'll take home is an empty game bag and a shoulder full of pain.

My lackluster ability to get a good return on the buckshot I send out to the skies above the dove fields makes me extra glad that the same thing cannot be said about God's Word. In Isaiah 55:11, the Lord said, "So will My word be which goes forth from My mouth; it will not return to Me empty, without accomplishing what I desire, and without succeeding in the matter for which I sent it." How thankful we all can be that when God shoots His words of truth, they always connect with the intended target. He never misses, and He will always have something to show for his efforts. The really great news, unlike a shotgun blast that's meant to take the life of a dove, is that God's words do not kill. Instead, they give life to the target that receives them.

Oh God, how grateful I am that, when You send forth the words of Your mouth, they connect precisely with the mark at which You aim. When my heart is Your target, and I am blessed with the life-altering truths that You let me understand, my spirit soars with life like a carefree dove in flight. I praise You for Your limitless skill with Your words. In the name of Your Word made flesh, Jesus Christ, amen.

36

Just a Smile

A cheerful look brings joy to the heart.

Proverbs 15:30 NLT

Two young hunting guides from different states met early in their careers while attending the same guide school. Since they shared a mutual passion for the outdoors, their friendship grew quickly. Upon completion of the course they both headed to Canada to work for the same outfitter.

One of the dynamics of the job they had heard about was how varied the personalities could be when it came to the hunters they would guide. Some were easygoing and a joy to lead. In most cases this was true because they came to the hunt with realistic expectations. They knew in advance that no matter how much cash was invested in a guided hunt, there's never a 100 percent guarantee that it will yield the trophy they hope to take home. For that reason there would be no blame or hard feelings to deal with if the hunt ends with an unpunched tag.

Some hunters, on the other hand, are not as understanding. If a hunt ends with nothing to show for their effort and monetary outlay, their reaction could be quite the opposite. These hunters were usually the ones who arrived at camp with the needle on their expectation meter slammed so far to the right that it wrapped around the peg and never fell out of the red zone. Consequently, if a guide failed to lead them to the animal they anticipated taking, they'd get increasingly irritable as the days passed.

As it turned out during the first week of bull moose season, the two friends' clients included both types of hunters. The adventure was to span six days, and the guide who was assigned the tightly wound hunter did his best to find a shooter that would satisfy all his hopes. As hard as he tried, however, the bullet clip in the hunter's rifle remained full through four days of the hunt, and the tension in the air was like a fog that grew increasingly thicker as the week went by. By Thursday they could report only one sighting of a bull that was much too young for the taking.

What made things even more tense was finding out at the end of day five that the guide's friend and his hunter had tagged a sixty-inch bull that morning. With that news the empty-handed hunter turned very quiet. During dinner it was obvious he was steaming mad. Before the meal was finished, angry words started flying.

As the irate hunter spewed his disappointment, the young newbie guide stood silent. His soul ached more and more with each verbal jab that was thrown at him. The oral beating was so severe that thoughts of abandoning his dream job and never coming back came to his mind. Then he looked at his friend across the room. What he saw was enough to help him survive the thrashing he was receiving. It was just a quick smile.

His friend's momentary grin seemed to say, "I have no doubt you did your best. Don't let this guy kill your spirit. We were warned about these kinds of hunters. Suck it up. Live and learn." And so he did. Later on, during deer season, he had a chance to return a healing smile when his buddy endured a word whoopin'.

It's true indeed that a "cheerful look brings joy to the heart" (Proverbs 15:30 NLT). The healing balm that can come with a timely smile can include the ingredients of acceptance, understanding, and approval. In the young guides' case, all of these blessings were needed and much appreciated. Is there someone in your life who could use a quick smile today?

Lord, what a wonderful gift You have given to mankind in our ability to form a cheerful look on our faces. I pray for Your help to be able to recognize when others are in need of my smile, and I thank You in advance for providing one for me in those times when I need it. You are a kind Father! Amen.

37

Cole Turkey

Be imitators of me, just as I also am of Christ.

1 CORINTHIANS 11:1

My friend Jason Cruise called me a couple of days before the start of the state's spring gobbler season and said, "Hey man, we gotta go knock a bird down together this year. Can you go Tuesday morning?"

Without hesitating, I said, "I'm in. Plan to come my way?"

I was more than willing to go turkey hunting with Jason not only because I enjoy his company, but he is extremely talented with all types of turkey calls. He can do more with a diaphragm mouth-type call than anyone I know, and his use of hand calls is remarkable. I know when I go with Jason, the gobblers are gonna come running to us like they're on a string.

Before we hung up, Jason added, "I'm bringing Cole with me. He won't be hunting, just tagging along. Are you okay with that?"

"No problem. How old is he now?"

"He's ten but he thinks he's seven." Then he said, "Dude, you know I'm kidding. You'll be amazed at how Cole can sit still."

I didn't doubt Jason's parenting skills and was sure his son wouldn't be a hindrance to the hunt. Later my assumption proved correct when the three of us met up at the farm, and young Cole answered, "Yes sir," when I asked him, "Are you ready to go chase some birds with us?" His respectful demeanor was refreshing.

As I anticipated, about ten o'clock that morning a pair of stubborn, lovesick gobblers fell victim to Jason's ability to make his hen calls sound irresistibly attractive. The full strutting male decoys he brought added an extra measure of enticement for the long beards to cross the huge field in which we were hunting. From nearly four hundred yards away the two mature birds hurried toward us, stopping occasionally to bloom into full strut and gobble loud and long. Five minutes later, two ten-inchers, each with over an inch and a quarter spurs, were headed to our skillets.

After the shots were fired, we enjoyed some vigorous high-fiving, took some pictures, watched the playback of the action on Jason's camera, and then took a short break before leaving for home. As we talked, Jason looked at his son and said to me, "Well, I know Cole learned a few things this morning about how to outsmart these old, intelligent birds. While you were watching the first gobbler that came in, I watched him. His eyes were so big I was afraid the birds would see 'em."

When we got back to our trucks, Jason said, "Thanks, man, for letting me bring Cole along. He saw some behavior this morning he can imitate, and I'm not just talking about things like watching you move only when the gobbler's eyes were hidden behind his full fan or being patient enough to let him come on in close so your kill shot would be quick and sure."

Jason paused and looked affectionately at his boy. "I'm talking about more important things like keeping your conversation G-rated, clean humor, showing an obvious passion for God's creation, and being willing to share your love of it with a young guy. He'll remember this day, and I will too."

I thanked Jason for his comments, shook hands with him and Cole, said good-bye and headed home. As I drove and reflected on the hunt I realized the greatest opportunity I had that morning was not putting one more long beard (which I called the Cole Turkey) in my record book; it was having the chance to be a positive influence in a young man's life. It motivated me to want to always be able to say what the apostle Paul said: "Be imitators of me" (1 Corinthians 11:1).

If those four words had been the extent of Paul's claim, it would have been nothing more than prideful boasting. But he quickly revealed his humble attitude when he added, "just as I am of Christ." Paul knew that his sole qualification for being a man anyone would want or need to imitate was his relationship with Christ. He's not the only one aware of that reality. I know it too, and Jason knows it as well. Someday, no doubt, Cole will also know it.

Father in heaven, I'm grateful for every opportunity You give me to be an example of Your grace, especially to the young ones in my life. I know I'd be foolish to ever say, "Be an imitator of me" without adding "as I imitate Christ," because without Your influence on my behavior, I would have no right to impact others. In the name of Christ, the one who is, above all, worthy to be imitated, amen.

38

The Boars

The name of the LORD is a strong tower;
The righteous runs into it and is safe.

PROVERBS 18:10

Before daylight came, my friend Don and I were standing side by side in a field on his Indiana property. Our plan was to split up and go to different tree stands, but before we did, Don had a question for me.

"Did you bring a pistol?"

I could barely see his face in the darkness, but I thought I saw a look of concern when I answered, "Uh, no. Why?"

That's when he broke the news that not far away was another farm that had been the home of some Russian boars. Though they were penned, the authorities hassled the man about keeping them, and his reaction to the matter was to release them.

The entire group dispersed and began to multiply. Needless to say, word quickly got around that the sizable hogs could be aggressive toward people.

I went silent for a few seconds as I cautiously looked around the open meadow. Completely surrounded by darkness and feeling vulnerable, I assumed my voice trembled a little when I said, "Brother, I somehow missed the memo about bringing a pistol. All I have is this compound bow. Should we go back and get something better for self-defense?"

"Naw. I think you'll be fine. We have radios. Let's turn them on, and you can call me just before they eat your last arm." Then he laughed. I laughed too, but nervously.

The sun would soon be lighting the skies, so we had to move. Reluctantly I said, "Okay. Do you think it's about a ten-minute walk for me?"

I could hear a smile in Don's voice when he answered, "Ten at the most. And don't worry about the boars. I'm yet to see one on my farm. But, still, you might want to hurry."

And hurry I did. I turned a ten-minute walk into a five-minute scurry and a time of prayer. I made plenty of noise as I rushed through the blackness of the predawn woods. I figured every deer in the area likely heard me, but I didn't care. My intent was to scare away any of the foreign fangs that might be feeding on Don's acorns, his grass, or the carcass of another hunter.

Needless to say, I was in a sweat by the time I returned to the top of the hill on the other side of a deep ravine. I quickly climbed into my stand feeling very happy to have all my appendages still attached. Then I radioed Don to see if he was still in one piece. He was, and I could hear he was still smiling.

I can laugh now about the dash I did through the woods to my Indiana tree stand. The thought of a pre-sunrise encounter with a pack of hungry Russian boars still gives me the heebie-jeebies. I'm not sure what I would have done, since I was woefully underpowered against pigs that, as far as I was concerned, were probably descendants of the herd that ran into the sea after Jesus cast a legion of demons into them.

It was amazing how unsafe I felt on the ground when I fought through the underbrush and stumbled over stumps and roots as I hurried to the ladder by the stand that morning. Equally amazing was how totally opposite my feelings were when I reached the top of the ladder and sat down on the stand seat. There, I completely relaxed, knowing I was in a place where I could not be attacked and become breakfast for the boars. The experience gave me a new appreciation for the good news found in Proverbs 18:10: "The name of the Lord is a strong tower; the righteous runs into it and is safe."

In Old Testament times, God's name was likened to a *migdal oz,* or an elevated, immensely fortified structure inaccessible to an enemy. The intent of the metaphor was to comfort the one who puts their trust in God with the fact that they have a place to run to when they're in danger. In God they are lifted up into the high place of His protection.

Since that morning in the Indiana woods, I have not looked at a tree stand in the same way. Now I consider it more than a place to enjoy the challenge of a deer hunt. It has become a reoccurring reminder that, in God, I have a safe place to go when the vicious boars of life pursue me. Whether its sudden sickness, fear of the future, financial woes, or anything else that may want to attack and destroy me, I can climb to safety by putting my trust in God. I hope you'll do the same.

God, thank You that You are willing and able to lift us up above the trouble of this life and set our spirits in a safe place. It's only in the mighty tower of Your name that I find peace, and for that reason I want to always live in such a way that I can confidently call on You with full trust that You will hear and save me. I know it's in Christ's name that I can come to you and ask these things, amen.

39

Two Safety Harnesses

God so loved the world, that He gave His
only begotten Son, that whoever believes in
Him shall not perish, but have eternal life.

JOHN 3:16

They say there are two types of hunters in the world:
those who have fallen out of a tree stand and those
who will. Because I can attest to the fact that tumbling out of an elevated stand can be a very painful
experience, no one has to talk me into strapping on
a safety harness when I go high up a tree.

Thankfully, I can say that my accident resulted
in injuries that were not life-threatening. My "still
around to tell about it" status compels me to urge
my fellow sportsmen to buckle up! The sad thing is,
though I am as clear about the need for the safety
device as I can be, there are those who choose to
ignore the idea. If I sense they think a harness is too

cumbersome, too expensive, or not necessary, I will sometimes try a different approach.

Instead of talking about the harness, I show them the scars on my left arm and talk about how long the searing pain lingered, as well as the back trouble that lasted for months. If that doesn't get their attention, I tell them a story or two about guys who've tumbled out of a tree stand and broken bones, ended up paralyzed, or worse, died due to their injuries. Usually the horror stories open their doubtful minds to the benefit of a safety harness.

The change of approach that sometimes has to be used when preaching about the need for hunters to consider a harness as a must item in their gear is similar to the preaching of the gospel. Sometimes, simply telling people they need Christ does little to get their attention, because they don't see *why* they need Him. For that reason, the message needs to be revamped.

Evangelist Ray Comfort offers some insight on how to help folks understand their need for Christ. He uses a well-known illustration about a parachute. For the sake of adapting it to the hunter's frame of reference, here's my version, using a safety harness instead of a parachute.

Suppose I handed you a state-of-the-art safety harness and said nothing more than, "I think you'd look good in this thing and you'll love it." But you don't care at all about how the thing looks on you, and you believe it could restrict your movement when you're up a tree. So you push it away and say, "Don't want it!"

But what if I handed you a harness and said, "Hey, man, I have it on good authority that when you go hunting tomorrow morning, you're going to make a terrible mistake that will result in your falling out of your tree stand. You'll break both legs and suffer a brain injury that will cause partial paralysis, and you'll lose your job because of it. For that reason, I got this safety harness for you to use."

Do you think your attitude about accepting the gift would change? No doubt it would because now you know *why* you need it. In a similar way, if you were someone who didn't believe you needed salvation through Christ, and I came to you and said, "I'd like to tell you about Jesus who died for your sins, you'll love Him," how open might you be to the message? Probably not much at all, if any, because I failed to explain *why* you need Him. What if I conveyed the message in a way that did explain why you needed Him?

"I have it on the authority of the Word of God that you have an appointment with death. After that you will face judgment, at which time you will be held accountable for your sin. But I have some good news. The certificate of debt that you will be required to pay for your sins was nailed to the cross in Christ. He willingly bore all your transgressions. If you repent and accept the gift of His forgiveness, He will cover you with His righteousness. Then, when you stand before almighty God, who, by the way, does not allow unrighteousness in His presence, you will be found acceptable because what He will see is not your attempt at righteousness but that you have put on the robe of His Son's righteousness."

With this approach do you think you would more seriously consider your need for Christ? I would think so. The reality is that there's no way I can predict you will fall out of a tree stand and get seriously hurt or killed. But what I can tell you about your spiritual future is true, because it is based in God's Word. See the Scripture references below.

Just as your opinion of the safety harness can be changed by knowing it can save your life, your appreciation of the message of hope through Christ can change when you realize He can save your soul. As much as I hope you will wear a safety harness that can spare you from physical harm, I hope you choose to put on Christ, who can save you from spiritual destruction.

Thank You, O God, for giving me the gift of salvation through Your Son, Jesus. Without Him, I know I would be in grave and eternal danger. I do accept Him and the forgiveness He offers by allowing my sin to be carried on His shoulders all the way to the cross. I bless You for changing my mind and my heart about Him as well as His sacrifice for me. I will be forever grateful, in His name I pray, amen.

And it is appointed unto men once to die, but after this the judgment (Hebrews 9:27 kjv).

When you were dead in your transgressions and the uncircumcision of your flesh, He made you alive together with Him, having forgiven us all our transgressions, having canceled out the certificate of debt consisting of decrees against us, which was hostile to us; and He has taken it out of the way, having nailed it to the cross (Colossians 2:13,14).

I will greatly rejoice in the Lord,
My soul shall be joyful in my God;
For He has clothed me with the garments of
    salvation,
He has covered me with the robe of righteousness (Isaiah 61:10).

But put on the Lord Jesus Christ, and make no provision for the flesh, to *fulfill its* lusts (Romans 13:14).

40

Laws or Lives

Which one of you will have a son or an ox fall into a well, and will not immediately pull him out on a Sabbath day?

LUKE 14:5

Whenever I tell the following story about deer hunting with my son, Nathan, I always wonder how the listener is going to feel about a specific detail. So far no one has reacted negatively to it.

Nathan and I went to a farm on a warm September morning to bow hunt deer. He was new at archery hunting, and I was only a year or so into it and had not had success. As it turned out, on this hunt each of us arrowed our first whitetail.

After I tracked my deer to where it had fallen, I tagged it and headed to my truck to get some rubber gloves to wear while field dressing the carcass. When I rounded the corner of the field I saw my truck, a dead doe, and Nathan sitting on the ground and leaning against a tire.

As I got closer to him, I realized he was struggling to breathe. There was a distinct blueness around his lips that alerted me to the frightening fact he was having significant respiratory trouble. At that moment I wasn't sure of the cause of his labored breathing, but the symptoms were similar to reactions he'd had previously to cat dander, only this was much worse. I later learned that it was an asthmatic response to deer dander known as "deer epithelium."

We had no time to guess. I had an emergency on my hands. Without hesitating, I helped Nathan into the pickup, fired up the engine, turned on the air conditioner, and aimed toward the highway that led home.

At this point in the story, I look at my listener to see if there's a question in their eyes. If there is, I expect to hear them ask, "But what about the two dead deer? They were your first archery kills, plus you left the meat to spoil in the September heat!"

To date, no fellow hunters have inquired about the two whitetails I left in the field. While I suspect they might quietly wonder about the fallen deer, I believe I know why they never ask about them. In a similar situation, any hunter would have done what I did, and for the same reason. Though hunters have a self-imposed policy that we should never abandon a downed animal, obviously we'll break that rule when it comes to saving a human life.

The commendable attitude of putting the life of another before any rule is exactly what Jesus challenged the Pharisees to accept. Luke 14:1-7 described the time He went to the house of a Pharisee on a Sabbath to eat bread. The lawyers who were there watched Jesus closely. They were looking for anything in His behavior to complain about for the sole purpose of tripping Him up.

A man was there who was sick with dropsy (severe fluid retention, swelling, likely a heart condition). Whether the man had been planted by the Pharisees who were trying to catch Jesus healing (or working, in their opinion) on the Sabbath—or just hanging around, hoping to be healed, the fellow's need was obvious. Knowing what His watchers were thinking, Jesus asked the Pharisees and the lawyers if they thought it was lawful to heal a man on the Sabbath. Not one of them said a word.

Likely it was because they hoped Jesus would heal the sick man so they could condemn Him for violating the Sabbath law.

While the religious leaders remained silent, Jesus touched the man, healed him, and sent him on his way. Knowing they were not happy with what He had done, Jesus gave them an opportunity to cast off their pride by asking, "Which one of you will have a son or an ox fall into a well, and will not immediately pull him out on a Sabbath day?" (verse 5).

Of course, none of them would have left either their son or their ox in the well. Yet they remained silent. In that moment they had to consciously decide which was more important: laws or life. Sadly, when they refused to rejoice that the sick man had been healed and, instead, accused and condemned Jesus for having compassion and doing good, they revealed their extreme arrogance.

This disheartening encounter with such a ruthlessly religious attitude was not the only one Jesus had while He walked the earth. He was so repulsed by it that, on one occasion, He said to them, "Woe to you, scribes and Pharisees, hypocrites! For you are like whitewashed tombs which on the outside appear beautiful, but inside they are full of dead men's bones and all uncleanness" (Matthew 23:27). Knowing how much He disapproved in his day of how the Pharisees put law keeping before the healing of lives, and believing that His Spirit dwells with us now, wouldn't it behoove us to examine our hearts to see if we have the same arrogant attitude?

May God help us to never be guilty of putting laws before lives. It's to this godly end we pray the following prayer.

Oh Father of mercy, I know You are not pleased if I place more value on religious rules than the precious souls around me who are spiritually in need of being rescued and healed. Please forgive me if I've been guilty of making a law out of anything that has to do with Your teachings. Instead, help me to always show Your great grace and mercy to those who are lost or hurt or who are trapped in the deep well of sin. Help me to be as gracious to them as You have been to me. In Your Son's holy name, amen.

41

Possibilities

> Come, see a man who told me every-
> thing I did. Could this be the Messiah?
>
> JOHN 4:29 NIV

I went to the woods a little earlier than usual to move my portable tree stand to another location before the deer began their evening feeding ritual. I did it for one simple reason: possibilities.

Nothing can cause me to detach a climber and move it to a different spot quicker than the conviction that another location holds more promise for success. Sometimes the move can be motivated by the discovery of more deer signs elsewhere or a report from another hunter about a sighting. On this day, however, the possibility factor came strongly into play because of what I had seen during the morning hunt: four sizable deer entering a thicket, where I assumed they would bed down. If my guess was right, when evening came they would exit where they entered, and if I was nearby, I might get a chance at taking one of them home. Thus the moving of the tree stand.

As it turned out, it was a smart thing to change locations because doing so yielded results. The family that received the forty-plus pounds of doe meat was especially grateful for the outcome. For me, the day's harvest was more proof that, as a hunter, I can be driven by possibilities, but it's a motivation that's not limited to the woods.

There've been other times when I've heard the whisper of the challenge, "Why not go over there and see what might happen?" That quiet call was the reason I decided to move from West Virginia to Tennessee and eventually marry my wife, Annie. To briefly explain, after I was discharged from the navy at twenty-two, I lived at home with my parents. While there, my interest in music stirred my curiosity about the city that is known for both making melodies and making a living at it. Wondering what I might find there, I pulled up stakes and headed to Nashville.

I didn't go directly to Music City, however. The adventure took me on a prolonged detour through

Kentucky, but after a few months I landed in Nashville. A friend and fellow musician joined me, and along with our day jobs, we started a Christian music group. The trio included a native Nashvillian we met after we arrived.

We sought guidance from the pastoral staff of the church we attended. One of the elders came to our apartment one evening to talk and pray with us about our future. During his prayer he asked God to lead each of us to good helpmates. Though I initially resisted the idea of marriage, several days later, somewhere in my heart, I heard, "Maybe you should go somewhere and pray about this possibility for a few days." So I did.

Enter Annie.

I went back to West Virginia to seek the Lord's direction about what the church elder had prayed about. Lo and behold, guess who had moved back to town after being in Philadelphia for two years. It was the very lovely and talented girl I had known in high school, Anne Williamson. Feeling drawn to the idea of finding out more about her, I did some self-coaxing. Finally I decided to ask her out for the purpose of exploring the possibilities.

During our date I was surprised to learn that,

after college and a couple of years of working in the inner city, she had decided to move back to the family farm. We spent some concentrated time together over the next few days, and then I headed back to Nashville.

To condense the story, after I left, Annie sensed a call in her heart to see what might happen in Tennessee. In November 1974 she said farewell to her family and moved to Music City. We dated a whole week, got engaged, and then married the following March. I can report that neither of us ever regretted responding to the possibilities.

Even more important than the two course-altering changes I've mentioned, there's another pursuit of a possibility that totally transformed my future.

When I realized I was a sinner in need of a Savior, it was good news to hear that a man called Jesus had died for the sake of my redemption. The message was similar to that of the woman whose story is told in John 4.

After meeting Jesus at a water well and discovering He was accepting of her in spite of her questionable past, she went back to town and said, "Come, see a man who told me everything I did. Could this be the Messiah [or Savior]?" (verse 29, NIV). Her message was filled with possibilities for those who heard, and many of them responded to it just as I did when I heard that Christ was my hope for salvation. I'll be forever grateful that I was prompted by the possibility of hope to move from my lost condition to the safety of a relationship with Christ.

If the move I made is one you have made as well, you know the joy of the decision. If you haven't made the move, I hope you'll respond when you hear, "Come, see a man…" The possibilities are endless!

Thank You, oh Father, for the possibilities for peace that are available to me through Your Holy Son, Jesus. I pray for the courage to make the move to Him. I bless You for Your grace that can eternally deliver me from darkness to the light of Your protective love. In Christ's name, amen.

42

Say Jesus

But seeing the wind, [Peter] became
frightened, and beginning to sink,
he cried out, "Lord, save me!"

MATTHEW 14:30

The television news report was heartrending to
watch. The anchor's face was somber as he reported
that 150 souls were on board a commercial flight
that crashed in a remote region of the French Alps.
The world eventually learned that the crash was
caused intentionally by the copilot.

A week after the disaster, news stations were
still covering the story. The fate of the victims was
still on my mind when I went to a nearby farm for
opening day of our spring turkey season. While sitting quietly in a field, I began to think about what
the passengers must have felt when they realized

the dreadful danger they were in. What did they say to themselves in those moments? I wondered if some of them were so stunned in that instant, they could think of only one word to say: "Jesus!" If so, was it meant as profanity? Likely not. Instead, it was most likely a desperate prayer.

I base my assumption on how many times I've heard people say the name of Jesus in moments of crisis. For example, on more than one occasion, Annie has whispered His name when one of our children was hurt. My dad has said it when I called him with the news that a grandchild had been rushed to the hospital. And I, too, have whispered the name of Jesus on several occasions, such as the day I received the gut-wrenching news that a good friend had suffered a heart attack.

With the likelihood in mind that some passengers on the ill-fated flight cried out the name of Jesus as their only prayer, and with the personal examples I could remember, I felt compelled to write a song. My intent was to encourage anyone who might suddenly be faced with a situation that threatens either body or soul or both and know that it's acceptable to simply say the name of Jesus. I can testify that it's the most effective prayer anyone can pray.

Say Jesus

In this world you will have tribulation
Clouds of fear may hover over you
You might try to pray, but you don't know
    what to say
In that moment there's one thing you can do
Just say, "Jesus!"
There is comfort in the whisper of His name
He's more than just a word; He's the reason
    you'll be heard
By the Father who knows all you're saying
When you just say, "Jesus!"

Don't forget about that night on stormy
    waters
The Savior's friends were sinking in despair
Then He came walking on the waves
And said, "It's Me, don't be afraid."
Oh, He's still enough when He's your only
    prayer
Just say, "Jesus!"

There is comfort in the whisper of His name
He's more than just a word; He's the reason
    you'll be heard
By the Father who knows all you're saying
When you just say, "Jesus!"*

---

*   Steve Chapman, Times & Seasons Music, Inc., BMI 2015.

43

The Third Grader's Question

Always be prepared to give an answer
to everyone who asks you to give the
reason for the hope that you have.

1 PETER 3:15 NIV

I received an email from a young girl that contained the following message:

Dear Mr. Chapman,

I'm in the third grade and I am doing my book report on your book, *A Look at Life from a Deer Stand*. I liked it and…I have a few questions for you. When did you go deer hunting in this story? And how did you come up with this wonderful story to tell?

I felt deeply honored that a third grader would choose to use one of my books for her report. For that reason I gladly provided answers to the two questions she asked, but there was an additional request in her message that deserved a response and required some extra thought:

I also have something else to ask of you. I'm trying to tell my friends at school about God. Sometimes I can't do it because we either don't have time or they aren't interested. Please help me.

I was moved and challenged by the fact that a young girl had such a strong desire to share her faith. After prayerfully considering what to say, here's how I responded:

You are so right that so many people these days are simply not interested in hearing about God. One reason might be they don't feel they need Him. If all their physical and social needs are met (food, clothing, place to stay, family, friends, etc.) and if they don't believe their sins are a problem in terms of their eternal destiny, then why would they be concerned enough to hear about God, about His care for them, and about His Son who died for their redemption?

While it's not true for everyone, very often it's

not until something tragic or sad happens that a person becomes interested in God and the help He can be to them. It could be sickness, the death of a family member or friend, a betrayal, feeling intensely alone, their parents' divorcing, or some other tragedy. If trouble comes and they realize they need God's help, they're more likely to turn to Him. Very often the first step they take toward God is by going to someone they believe is one of His followers. With this in mind, there are some very important things you can do.

Get to know God as deeply as you can, and the best way to do that is through the study of His written Word. His Word will teach you how to be trustworthy, how to keep good morals, how to be friendly and helpful. If your ambition is to please the Lord, He will see to it that you'll be someone your friends can turn to when they realize they need to hear about God.

One other suggestion is to pray for your friends every day. Ask God to open the door for you to share Him with them, and then be ready to speak on His behalf when they ask. Memorize the following verse and let it be your determination in regard to testifying to your friends of God's grace:

> But in your hearts revere Christ as Lord. Always be prepared to give an answer to everyone who asks you to give the reason for the hope that you have. But do this with gentleness and respect, keeping a clear conscience (1 Peter 3:15-16 NIV).

I sent my response to the email address provided by the young girl and realized, when I received a reply about an hour later that it went straight to her teacher. I was thrilled (and relieved) to read her sincere thanks for taking the time to answer her student's questions about the book. Then she said that she was a woman of faith and mentioned how much she longed to offer the kind of spiritually based instruction I had given her student but couldn't do so in the school where she worked. She was thrilled that the child had contacted me directly as the author of the book she was reading because my reply was acceptable information for her student to include in the report. May God be praised!

I hope this story reminds you of three encouraging facts. One, there are young people in our chaotic times who have a passion for the good news of God and sincerely desire to share it with others. Two, there are teachers in our schools who are concerned not only with the academic needs of their students but also their spiritual needs. And three, anyone who truly wants to share God with others can anticipate the opportunity to do it. Why? The answer is implied in the Bible verse I sent the inquisitive third grader: "Always be prepared to give an answer" (verse 15). That doesn't sound like an "if they ask" situation. Instead, it sounds like a "*when* they ask" alert. Will you be ready?

God, thank You for every opportunity You give me to share Your goodness with others. Help me to notice when You've opened the door, and give me the words to say when it happens. Also, thank You for the zeal of others, especially the young ones, who want to tell people about You. I pray for some of that fervor to be my own. In Christ's name, amen.

44

The Blessing of Darkness

Your light will rise in the darkness.

ISAIAH 58:10

If I'm fortunate enough to live the nearly twenty-six thousand days of the average life span, I calculate that, as a hunter, I will have entered the woods before sunrise on around 10 percent of them. That represents a lot of time dealing with darkness and the hazards that go with it, including tripping over tree roots, stepping into holes hidden under leaves, being trapped in humongous spider webs I couldn't see, and fighting the eerie feelings that predawn blackness can bring.

Though I'm not a huge fan of the dark, due to the added challenges it brings to hunting, I've learned to appreciate it for two reasons. When it comes to outsmarting the critters I'm after, sneaking into their neighborhood under the cover of darkness gives me an advantage that has often paid off. For example, setting up a camo pop-up blind in an open field during turkey season is much better done before daylight. Otherwise, the nearby birds would see me and bust me before I had a chance to bust any of them.

Second, I've come to value the dark because of something I heard in a sermon. To paraphrase the pastor: "There's no need to fear darkness. It can't hurt you. All the darkness in the universe can't extinguish the light in the flame of one small candle. Besides"—and this is what especially caught my ear—"think about what good has come from darkness."

Reading Genesis 1:2-5 the pastor reminded us, "The earth was formless and void, and darkness was over the surface of the deep, and the Spirit of God was moving over the surface of the waters. Then God said, 'Let there be light'; and there was light. God saw the light was good; and God separated the light from the darkness. God called the light day, and the darkness He called night."

The pastor then said:

"It was out of darkness that light came. But please wait—there's more! John 12:24 reveals an amazing process that takes place in the darkness below the surface of the ground. Consider the fact that 'unless a grain of wheat falls into the earth and dies, it remains alone; but if it dies, it bears much fruit.' It's an amazing and mysterious transformation that takes place in the dark. But that's not all—there's more!

"Look at John 20:1. It says, 'Now on the first day of the week Mary Magdalene came early to the tomb, while it was still dark, and saw the stone already taken away from the tomb.' The gloomy darkness of the burial tomb that had held the crucified body of Christ could not contain His resurrected body. In the way that our temporary lives came forth from the darkness of our mother's womb, life eternal came forth from the pitch-black confines of the tomb. What an incredible reminder that darkness, in the positive sense of the word, is a blessing if we understand that it will always yield to the Light of the World. But wait—there's one more thing."

As tenderly as the pastor could say it, he encouraged everyone in the room by adding, "What dark place do you feel you're in right now? Is your family in disarray, has your job security turned doubtful, are you at odds with a friend, have you gotten a scary diagnosis? Whatever form that darkness has taken in your life, remember that God can use it to give birth to something good. He's done it before. He can do it again!"

Perhaps the next time you enter the woods before the sun comes up, and you're sitting quietly in the dark, waiting excitedly for the light, you'll remember how God, and God alone, can turn darkness into a blessing for those who love Him.

God of all light, how grateful I am that You are fully able and willing to bring light out of darkness and life out of death. I pray that You will take the darkness that I'm facing and use it to bring glory to Yourself. In the bright and blessed name of Jesus, amen.

45

Straying Beagle

Therefore I was angry with this generation,
and said, They always go astray in their
heart; and they did not know my ways.

HEBREWS 3:10

The hillside looked very "rabbit-ish" to me as my
friend and I worked our way through the waist-
high brush and briars. Besides the sound of the
thorns ripping at our overalls, the only thing we
could hear was the grunt-like snort of the beagle
that had its nose to the ground sniffing excitedly
for the hint of cottontail. Then all heaven broke
loose.

To my ear there's hardly anything as sweet sounding as the bellow of a beagle that has just picked up
the scent of a rabbit. The moment it happened, I
knew without a doubt the dog was happy and I

213

too was beyond happy with the realization that the chase was on. All my senses came to full alert as I positioned myself and waited for the rabbit to eventually make his typical full-circle run in front of the beagle and come back to where I stood waiting with my thumb on the shotgun safety.

But this chase sounded different. Usually when a running rabbit makes its predictable sweeping turn, the bark of the beagle will change from a somewhat muffled, going-away tone to a more distinct I'm-headed-your-way tone. The excitement I anticipated with the change was much too delayed, and worry began to replace the thrill I was feeling.

After several minutes of listening, the dog's bark faded into the distance. My friend and I both knew he had topped the hill and was descending into the next hollow. That's when owner of the dog spoke with fiery anger in his few words.

"That stupid dog is on a deer again!"

We waited another few minutes, and suddenly my friend took off up the hillside in a huff. The long, briary arms of the tangled brush were no match for the furious bulldozer he had become. Because the beagle had gotten on the trail of a whitetail and gone out of earshot of his attempts to call it back, he was on a mission of retrieval. At that point, I feared that the hunt was over.

As it turned out, I was right. It took a while for my friend to reconnect with the dog, and by then he was upset enough that he brought the hunt to an abrupt end. We went home without a single rabbit to show for our efforts. However, I did take something of value away from the hunt. I got a really good picture of who I *don't* want to be when it comes to my walk as a disciple of Christ.

I don't want to displease or disappoint Him by allowing myself to be so enticed by sin that I stray from the trail of righteousness. While I trust in His grace to forgive me when it happens, I'd rather strive to keep the attitude that the apostle Paul had as stated in 2 Corinthians 5:9. "Therefore we also have as our ambition, whether at home or absent, to be pleasing to Him."

Father in Heaven, thank You for loving us even when we fail You by wandering off the path You have taught us to follow. Your great kindness and

forgiveness in those times is all the
more reason to want to never be so
easily drawn aside from Your ways.
I ask for Your help to not stray from
You in my heart. May it be so to Your
glory and to that alone. In Your name
I pray.

46

Food for Naught

*Nothing outside a person can defile
them by going into them.*

MARK 7:15 NIV

My parents, P.J. and Lillian Chapman, were invited to submit recipes for a cookbook that was to be sold as a fund-raising project by the ladies at a church in their area. Since my parents were friends with the women who were screening the contributions, they mischievously sent a joke recipe along with several others. They never dreamed it would be included in the compilation and even end up as one of the readers' favorites. The following is the joke recipe.

P. J.'s Breakfast Sandwich

2 Slices whole white bread
1-inch Sliced bologna, chopped

1 Large egg, scrambled
2 Tablespoons real mayo
2 Thick slices of homegrown tomato
Pinch of salt
Tad of pepper
1 Tall glass of whole milk

Grease iron skillet with lard. Combine egg and bologna in a cereal bowl and mix slightly. Add salt and pepper. Pour into hot skillet and fry until done. Slather mayo on one slice of bread and add tomatoes. Lay scrambled egg and bologna slab on the bread and top it with the second slice. Press gently with palm of hand. Stand in front of the kitchen window and hold sandwich over the sink so the mayo won't drip on the floor. Look out the window, watch the traffic, occasionally wipe the mayo off your mouth, and wash it all down with the milk. Rinse your false teeth in the sink, and then go back and lay on the couch.

Like many others, I laughed out loud when I read this recipe, but not just because of its hilarious imagery. I laughed because I've seen my Dad do exactly what the recipe says. I've seen the mayo drip to the floor. I've observed when he needed two napkins to wipe his mouth.

I realize that some health-conscious people might feel a little nauseated by the description of Dad's culinary creation. They would never consider consuming such a sandwich. If you're one of them, I understand how you feel, but I have some news that may be extra disturbing. I've stood next to Dad at the kitchen sink after he carefully halved one of his deadly delights and shared in the joyful, tasty experience (minus the denture-cleaning part).

Before you scratch my name off your list of those you consider sane, I want to add that my consuming concoctions like my father's breakfast sandwich is something that rarely happens. I might occasionally lift my self-imposed dietary restrictions while at a deer hunting camp or in a duck blind, where cooking and eating are done with no regard to potential arterial blockage. But when I do, I don't have to feel guilty about it for two reasons. One, I have no plans to make the indulgence a habit, and two, because of what Jesus said in Mark 7:14-16: "Listen to me, everyone, and understand this. Nothing outside a person can defile them by going into him. Rather, it is what comes out of a person that defiles them" (NIV).

Jesus said this in front of some Pharisees and teachers of the law who complained that His disciples had eaten with unclean, unwashed hands. Knowing that their pre-meal ceremonial hand washing (as well as the ritual washing of their cups, pitchers, and kettles) was nothing more than a display of their "better than you" attitude, Jesus used the situation to reveal their hypocrisy. To drive the point home, He quoted the prophet Isaiah: "These people come near to me with their mouth and honor me with their lips, but their hearts are far from me. Their worship of me is based on merely human rules they have been taught" (29:13 NIV).

After the Pharisees had gone, Jesus privately elaborated by telling His followers: Don't you see that nothing that enters a person from the outside can defile them? For it doesn't go into their heart but into their stomach, and then out of the body... What comes out of a person is what defiles them. For it is from within, out of a person's heart, that evil thoughts come—sexual immorality, theft, murder, adultery, greed, malice, deceit, lewdness, envy, slander, arrogance and folly. All these evils come from inside and defile a person (Mark 7:18-19 NIV).

The Lord's words sure do put my dad's breakfast sandwich in perspective in terms of what's bad for me. I need to be much more concerned about what proceeds from my heart than what goes into my belly. Hopefully you feel the same way. If so, the next time you treat yourself to something from the "Are You Sure You Should Eat That?" menu, you'll be reminded to not worry so much about what you're putting in but what's coming out!

Dear God, thank You for food! What a blessing it is to enjoy it. As I do, I want to remember that You said it's not what goes into my belly that can hurt me but what comes out of my heart. I need Your help to keep my heart clean, because I know my spiritual health depends on it. In Your Son's holy name I pray, amen.

47

Only God

I, the LORD, am the maker of all things.

ISAIAH 44:24

The four-hour horseback ride behind my guide took us through some dense and dark timber as we headed up a Montana mountain. Being new to sitting for hours in a leather saddle, the climb was quite a test on my yet-to-be-calloused backside, but the payoff was worth it. When we came to a clearing that allowed me my first view of the vastness of the territory, I was stunned.

For a few minutes my focus on the impending elk hunt turned into a sight of the wide valley below. Miles away I could see snow-capped mountains that rose to form the far wall of the deep valley, and behind them were even higher peaks that seemed to extend forever into the distance. To this day my first view of the magnificent Montana vista remains one of my favorite outdoor memories.

I remember what I said when my eyes beheld the incredible scenery. It was a two-word declaration I had used before, when I saw an unforgettable Middle Tennessee sunrise or the golden evening sun that lit up the rich fall colors on the trees on our rolling hills. This time, however, the surprising immensity of the western territory prompted me to say the words just a little louder.

"Only God!"

It was as if the statement came from deep in my soul, somewhere as deep as the mountains were high. It was a moment of praise, not to praise what I was seeing, but to praise Him who had made what I was seeing.

It felt really good to respond to the extraordinary sight with, "Only God!" I suppose I could have used more words, but the two seemed enough. I was confident He knew it was my way of agreeing with Him when He said, "I, the LORD, am the maker of all things, stretching out the heavens by Myself and spreading out the earth all alone" (Isaiah 44:24).

Before I turned my horse to follow the guide on up the mountain, I gave one more look at this awesome view. And one more time I said it out loud: "Only God!" When I did, I felt in my soul that He smiled.

God, I admit that You can't be compared to anyone, especially when it comes to Your creative ability. You have no equal in this universe. Only You, God, can give such a tangible sign of Your majesty and power as You've given through creation. I will bless Your name now and always for it, in Christ's name, amen.

48

The Deadly Look Back

Remember Lot's wife.

LUKE 17:32

When my son and I went to the Cheyenne, Wyoming, area to hunt, it was our first time to pursue a species of deer we had only seen in photos. We were excited about having an encounter with one of the state's big-bodied mule deer.

During the ride from the airport to our host's farm, we asked him to give us some tips on hunting in his neck of the prairie. One of the things he told us turned out to be a vital piece of information in terms of having a successful hunt. We were all ears as he spoke.

"I don't know what your whitetail deer do in the east when you spook 'em, but if you happen to spook a big mulie out here and he runs off, don't just stand there gawking at 'im. If he's a buck you want to take, while he's running, you'll want to quickly get your gun to your shoulder, find him in the scope, and be ready to take a shot. The reason is, more times than not a mulie will run a little and then stop, turn around, and look your way. It's a character trait that has sent a lot of 'em to the skillet."

Sure enough, just like he said, we saw more than one mule deer shoot out of a bedding spot, bounce away in front of us like a giant rabbit as they headed up a grassy hillside, and then stop for their typical look back. One of them, a tall and impressive four by four that looked rather obese, made the deadly mistake of responding to his nature. When he momentarily halted his escape and turned to look back, it was lights out for him.

When I recall the sight of the Wyoming mule deer coming to a dead stop and looking back, I often do what is suggested in Luke 17:32. I "remember Lot's wife" who chose to ignore the warning given to the Lot family to not look back while fleeing their home in Sodom. As a result of her willful disobedience, she turned into a standing salt lick.

While the Genesis account of what happened to Lot's wife does not reveal the reason she turned around, I assume it was more than mere curiosity. It's safe to say that something or someone left behind pulled at her heart. Whatever attachment she had to Sodom would have been better abandoned. If she would have kept her eyes straight ahead and kept running, she would have saved her life.

Because God wisely never wastes a good illustration, He saw to it that Mrs. Lot's story got a mention in the New Testament. The Luke 17 reference to her fateful decision to look back is an intentional and timeless warning to all of us: "On that day no one who is on the housetop, with possessions inside, should go down to get them. Likewise, no one in the field should go back for anything. Remember Lot's wife! Whoever tries to keep their life will lose it, and whoever loses their life will preserve it" (verses 31-33 NIV).

For most of us, holding our possessions and connections to this life with a wide-open hand is much easier said than done. But how glad we'll be that we are untethered to the temporal things of this world on the day Christ returns and we fly away with Him.

Father in heaven, I need Your help to daily live with an open-hand attitude when it comes to earthly possessions and my connections to this life. I am grateful for all You've provided for me in this world, but when I hear Your call, I don't want to be so tightly tethered to it that I would look back and miss what You have prepared for me in heaven. In Christ's name I pray, amen.

49

Signals

I will lift up my eyes to the mountains;
From where shall my help come?

PSALM 121:1

At the invitation of a gentleman who was at a concert that Annie and I did, I traveled to Prescott, Arizona, to bow hunt the elusive javelina boar. I had only two days to tag this "desert ghost," and we hunted hard with no sightings until the second afternoon. Then about four o'clock we sat down on a ridge to glass a deep ravine and the hill on the other side of it. After a few minutes of scanning the brushy ground, I heard some welcome words from my new friend and guide, Richard.

"I see a group of pigs near the ridge on the other side of this ravine."

My heart rate increased and then doubled when he said, "We don't have a whole lot of time left, but you might be able to get close to them if you want to try."

I was more than willing and asked what I could do.

"If you can hurry and get up on the other side of this hill, I can signal you to where the pigs are. Every two or three minutes, look at me through your binoculars. I'll give you signals to go up, right, left, et cetera. Then if I think you're close enough to get a shot, I'll act like I'm pulling on a bowstring. That's when you'll need to knock an arrow and be ready to shoot!"

He didn't have to coax me to give the idea a try. I took off down into the ravine. About twenty-five minutes later, I was high enough on the other side to glass Richard for the first time, and he gave me the "go up" signal. After another twenty minutes of climbing and following his hand signals to keep going up and to my right, I reached the ridge of the hill. I stopped to take another look at my guide through my binoculars. What I saw him doing put me on high alert.

Silhouetted against the Arizona sky, I saw Richard frantically and repeatedly yanking at his air bow. His quick movements told me the small herd of javelina was closing in fast. As I let go of my binoculars and ripped an arrow out of my quiver, I suddenly smelled pigs. It was the distinct, pungent odor Richard had told me I might smell if the ghosts were close.

Ten seconds later I saw a hefty male boar making his way toward me on what appeared to be a trail. When the fifty-pounder was about fifteen yards from me, he stopped dead in his tracks. He was obviously surprised to see a human standing in his way. I was already at full draw when he appeared, and as he turned to run I closed the deal. He didn't go but ten yards before expiring.

Today, the mounted head and shoulders of my first and only javelina is in my possession. Each time I look at it, I remember every detail of the hunt and still feel the excitement I felt the day I tagged him. I also think of the ingenious idea Richard had to signal me to the prize. I was amazed at how well it worked. It's a tactic I've since seen used by other guides who, because walkie-talkies are not permitted in an area, have signaled their hunters to their trophies.

Psalm 121:1 comes to mind when I think of the visual exchange between Richard and me. I needed Richard's help, so I kept looking up the mountain.

I didn't watch the four-footed prize I was after because I couldn't see him. Richard had the bigger, wider view of the area, and for that reason I had to depend on my guide in order to have success.

In a very similar way, Jesus has a view of this world that I don't have. He sees the details of time and space, and no doubt it's for that reason that He wants all of us to look heavenward for our help. We can do just that through the binoculars of His written Word. I know if I respond to the signals He provides in those pages, the day will come when I'll get the ultimate prize of being eternally safe in His presence. May it be so for you as well.

Thank You, Jesus, that You care enough about me to lead me to spiritual success. Help me remember to always be looking Your way for guidance. I need Your signals to know where to go and when to be ready for the awesome moment You appear. In Your name I pray, amen.

50

Margaret's Horse

The fear of the LORD is the beginning of knowledge.

PROVERBS 1:7

When my son, Nathan, and I went to Montana to elk hunt with guide Randy Petrich, we were blessed to ascend the tall mountains on horseback. Because my limited experience in a saddle included a near tragedy many years earlier, mounting up that first morning of the hunt was a little nerve-racking.

My designated ride for the week was a coal black horse named Spook. Randy told me the animal was named for the way he seemed to disappear in the deep of night. He was right, because as I sat on Spook in the darkness of the stall at four o'clock in the morning, I could feel him under me but I could hardly see him. I felt like I was in nothing but a saddle hovering above the ground. It was eerie.

While Randy was getting Nathan's horse ready for him, my mind wandered to 1965. I recalled the day I went with my mother to a farm owned by her friend Margaret. I was fifteen and rather adventurous, so when Margaret suggested I explore the barn while she and Mother visited, I jumped at the chance.

There was not all that much to see except a couple of horses. One was just inside the fence, near the barn door. The other was about seventy-five yards away, grazing on some grass. I stepped inside the barn to see what I could find, and there on a rack was a saddle. I looked at it, then leaned out and looked around the barn door at the horse, then looked back at the saddle and whispered to myself, "Why not?"

I had watched enough episodes of *Gunsmoke* and *Bonanza* to have a vague idea of how to throw a saddle over a horse, so I grabbed the heap of nicely engraved leather just like the television cowboys did and walked over to the horse. He didn't seem to mind when the saddle landed on its spine.

I gripped the bridle he was wearing, led him to the fence, and then climbed up the rails high enough to put my leg over the horse's back. I sat down gingerly in the saddle and felt quite comfortable. For about twenty seconds I didn't move. Then, just as I'd seen Ben and all the Cartwright boys do, I poked the horse with my heels and shifted front and back a little to see if he would move forward.

He did!

I didn't have a rein to hold, so I grabbed the horse's mane and pulled it to the right. Amazingly, he turned in that direction and took about ten steps. At that moment his head came up, and he seemed to stare across a field for a few seconds. And then, all at once, with no warning, he broke into a full run toward the other horse. I assumed it was his girlfriend.

I squeezed my legs against the horse's ribs as tight as I could, but I quickly discovered one detail I had overlooked when I saddled him. I didn't know the straps attached to the saddle were supposed to go under the horse's belly to cinch it onto the horse. I was sitting on a completely loose saddle. Within a few yards I felt the saddle shifting to the right. Farther and farther it slid until, finally, I went with it all the way to the ground.

Thanks to the soft dirt I didn't break any bones or draw blood when I hit. But it was at least thirty seconds before I could breathe again. When I was sure I could stand, I got up and carried the dusty saddle back to the rack where I found it and headed to the house.

When my mother saw the dirt and grass stains on my pants and saw that I was a bit shaken, she asked what had happened.

I admitted what I had done and waited for the fallout from her as well as a scolding from Margaret. But when they realized I wasn't injured, Mom just shook her head, sat back in her chair, and said, "Live and learn."

Our hostess didn't say anything, but I could tell she was relieved we weren't on our way to a hospital.

What did I learn from my failed attempt to "ride 'em cowboy"? I discovered if I had approached Margaret's horse with a little fear and some wise respect for its power, it would have made me get some knowledge about how to handle him. That know-how would have spared me the fall that could have injured me. But I was clueless about how strong her nine-hundred-pound animal was, as well as how unpredictable a horse can be when handled by a stranger. I'm grateful I survived the fall and gained enough smarts to know the next time I want to get on something powerful like a horse (including metal ponies, like motorcycles), I better know some things about it before I do.

In the same way that respecting a horse can be the first step in becoming a smarter rider, embracing the fear of the Lord "is the beginning of wisdom" (Proverbs 1:7). God's immeasurable power with which He can do all things—"with God all things are possible" (Matthew 19:26)—is what behooves me to gain as much understanding of Him as I can. I can do this by studying His ways, knowing His desires for me, and learning how He wants me to live. It's the safest way to relate to Him.

By the way, Spook and I got along just fine during my week with him in the Montana mountains. I made it home in one piece.

Dear God, there is none greater or more powerful than You. Because this is absolutely true, I ask You to help me learn more about You through Your written Word, through prayer, and through fellowship with others whose hearts are filled with reverence for You. Thank You for being willing to let me get close to You and to ride safely on Your shoulders through the fields of this life. Blessed be Your precious and powerful name. In Christ I pray, amen.

51

Bad Sinners
Make Good Saints

It is a trustworthy statement, deserving full acceptance, that Christ Jesus came into the world to save sinners, among whom I am foremost of all.

1 TIMOTHY 1:15

The phone rang one day, around noon, in a home along a rural highway in an eastern state. The young man who answered took a deep breath and wondered if it was the call he had been waiting for. Sure enough, it was.

"Hello."

"Jim?"

Jim's voice sounded a little tentative when he answered, "Yes sir." He finally took a breath when he heard, "I have some good news for you. You can put the word *officer* in front of your name because you got the job. Welcome to the Department of Wildlife Resources team!"

Jim quietly congratulated himself with an arm pump and kept his voice calm as he said thanks for the news.

There was something the DWR didn't know about Jim that made him a unique new employee. Before he entered the training program that led to this position, he had become familiar with most, if not all, the tricks that poachers, trespassers, night hunters, illegal baiters, and other offenders used to bend or break the law. Also, he knew about the back roads and the kind of hideouts that were used to elude game wardens when they gave chase.

Jim didn't get the knowledge by studying a book, being an observer on a stakeout, or eavesdropping on conversations. Instead, he was knowledgeable of how bad guys operated because he had been one of them.

By the time he was twenty years old, he had hunted and trapped far more days out of season than in season than anyone he knew. He had killed more deer at night than in the daytime, and he ignored all the duck, turkey, and small game limits.

Plus, as far as he was concerned, the signs that said No Hunting or Trespassing were merely suggestions. It was a life he boasted about to his close friends, but then something happened that opened his eyes to the need for change.

While walking alone one night to a cave where he hid several of his traps, he was on a narrow trail he had cleared through a dense thicket. To avoid anyone knowing he was on the hillside, he didn't use a flashlight or a headlamp. Suddenly, about thirty yards ahead, he saw a light come on. It was so bright he was instantly blinded. Then he heard a voice amplified through a megaphone.

"Don't move, young man. I'm from the Department of Fish and Game, and I want you to lay down on the ground and put your hands behind your back."

Jim assumed he had bragged to one too many people about his exploits and that he was headed to jail. He had never felt an ounce of sorrow for how he lived, but suddenly he was drowning in fear and regret. His knees trembled as he fell to the dirt on the trail, and the dread of what was ahead felt like a tree had fallen on his heart.

Then he heard laughter.

Seeing Jim's face had turned pale and that he was nearly in tears, his friends decided it was time to let him know he had been pranked. They laughed at how obedient Jim was to the command to lay down on the ground. Of course, Jim didn't think it was all that funny. All he could feel was utter relief that he was not under arrest.

In the following days Jim tried to shake the prank off, but something about it haunted him. The deep remorse he felt when the light came on as he walked through the darkness had not gone away. He had never given much thought to spiritual things, but he wondered if God was involved with the feelings he was having.

He began to think about what would've happened if his two prankster friends had actually been authorities of the state. The more he thought about it, the stronger the feeling grew that he needed to stop his life of outdoor crime and find out more about how God wanted him to live. Otherwise, there'd likely be a real arrest, a conviction, and no doubt, some jail time in his future.

Within a week Jim gathered up his stash of traps,

bait boxes, spotlights, and all the other gear he used for law breaking and destroyed them. With a heart full of determination to do right by the game laws, he started down a different trail, one that eventually led him to become a Christian. It was not long after that, he responded to an advertisement about training for a job with the organization he had disrespected for so long.

After Jim started his job with the game commission, his superiors were impressed with how passionate he was about the work and how well he did it. What they didn't realize was that Jim's commitment to his job was related to how grateful he was that he had "seen the light" and could live worry-free. For that reason he wanted to work harder for the good guys than he worked as one of the bad guys.

If you haven't noticed by now, I'll point out that there is a striking resemblance between Jim's story and that of the apostle Paul's experience. Paul had worked against God for a long time by persecuting the followers of Christ. He even held the coats of the people who executed the deacon Stephen. Paul was a bad guy, that is, until he was on his way to Damascus and was blinded by a light and heard a voice speak.

God had cornered Paul, and now He had his undivided attention. As a result, the apostle spent a lot of sleepless nights dealing with the regret he revealed in his preaching and writings.

> As I punished them often in all the synagogues, I tried to force them to blaspheme; and being furiously enraged at them, I kept pursuing them even to foreign cities (Acts 26:11).

> I am the least of the apostles, and not fit to be called an apostle, because I persecuted the church of God (1 Corinthians 15:9).

Paul ended up working a lot harder for the right than he did the wrong. He credited God's grace for the reversal when he added, "I labored even more than all of them, yet not I, but the grace of God with me" (1 Corinthians 15:10).

Paul's radical conversion, as well as Jim's total change of heart, are two examples of what can happen when the bright light of God's grace helps sinners see who they really are. It's His mercy, and that alone, that can take sinners and make them good saints. Have you seen that light yet?

God, how grateful I am that You would love me enough to blind me with the light of the truth that I, too, have sinned and come short of Your glory. Take my life now and use it for the cause of righteousness. In Christ's name I pray, amen.

52

Listen to Your Guide

Listen to counsel and accept discipline,
That you may be wise the rest of your days.

PROVERBS 19:20

Around 1983 Annie and I flew to Alaska for the first time. The aerial view of the state was breathtaking to say the least. I remember looking at the incredibly vast territory and thinking about how much I would love to be somewhere down there, not as a musician, but as a hunter. The dream began during that first visit and continued through the years. I assumed it would remain a dream, and then one day, in my sixty-fourth year, a call came that I'll never forget.

A friend extended an invitation to join him and another hunter on a brown bear hunt. There are not enough pages in this book to describe how grateful I felt for the opportunity as well as what the trip was like. As I mentioned earlier, the ten-day trip yielded a brown bear over nine feet tall and weighing nearly a thousand pounds.

Of all the memories I enjoy recalling about that adventure, remembering my guide, the legendary Dale Adams, is extra special to me. His story telling was superb, his humor kept us all in stitches, his demeanor was very friendly, and he showed a ton of patience with answering the same questions that every newbie brown bear hunter feels compelled to ask. He always had a smile when he answered questions such as:

Q: "Where we gonna hunt today?"
A: "In Alaska!"

Q: "How far do those mountains go?"
A: "To the other side of the island."

Q: "How deep is the water in this inlet?"
A: "It goes all the way to the bottom."

Q: "Is that bear big enough to take?"
A: "Where to?"

As an outfitter, the single most valuable characteristic Dale possessed was his confidence as a brown bear guide. Simply put, the man knew what he was doing. He was as familiar with the territory as he was with the back of his weather-worn hands. For that reason, I felt very safe in his care.

Accompanying us on the hunt was my friend Lindsey Williams. He, too, was captivated by Dale's delightful personality. We both agreed that when the huge bear was walking down the beach toward us, there was no one else we'd rather have been close to than Dale. I was shaking like Barney Fife, and I'll never forget how Dale helped bring some calm to my nerves as he verbally walked me through the shot process. His voice never waivered with tension the way mine did. Lindsey was within earshot, behind a video camera, and he, too, felt safe in Dale's care.

If you were headed to Alaska to hunt a monster bear and asked me for my number-one bit of advice, I'd tell you, "Listen to your guide!" It's the smartest thing I did while I was there.

Because Lindsey and I were so enamored with Dale Adams, we decided to give him the gift of a song. Our intent was to honor the legend that he is. The lyric was written on the boat the day after

I tagged the bear. We got some help from his wife, Lori, who gave us some tips about the lingo used in the brown bear guiding world. Here're the lyrics to "Big Brown Bear."

Big Brown Bear

Big brown bear
He knows where they are and he'll take you
    there
Way up north
To the last frontier
He'll help you find a big brown bear
Big brown bear
Big brown bear
He'll get you one with thick dark hair
The wind and tide
They never play fair
But he'll push through for a big brown bear
Stovepipe nose
Washtub head
Big 'ol stud, Alaska-fed
Hit 'im once
Hit 'im again
Hit 'im till you see Dale Adams grin

Big brown bear
Big brown bear
Coal black eyes, can you feel his stare?
Listen to your guide
No need to be scared
And you'll be wearin' that big brown bear.*

Lindsey and I hoped our poetic rendering of our impression of Dale was sufficient thanks to him for making our trip so incredibly memorable. But there's a compliment of even greater depth he deserves. That is, Dale's role as a hunting guide is an earthly picture of what God our heavenly guide is like. God knows what He's doing. He's totally trustworthy. His stories are unforgettable. His presence is a joy. He's very patient with newbies (and oldies too!). And where He lives is beyond awesome.

One difference between Dale and God that Dale would want you to know is that while his success rate is impressively high when it comes to his hunters getting their big trophies, God's percentage rate with His hunters of truth is always 100 percent. So if you're looking for a big brown bear, call Dale. If you're looking for the truth, call on God!

---

*   Steve Chapman and Lindsey Williams, Times & Seasons Music, BMI, Really Big Bison Productions, SESAC, 2015.

Thank You, God, for being my eternal guide. I want to follow You, listen closely to Your instructions, and trust You every step of the way. In Your Son's name I pray, Amen.

Song Credits

"The Assistant Guide," Alex Carter, 2015. Used by permission.

"Believe It to See It," Steve Chapman, Lindsey Williams, and Kenna Turner West, Times & Seasons Music, Inc., BMI, Really Big Bison Productions, SESAC, Daywind Music, BMI, 2013.

"Big Brown Bear," Steve Chapman and Lindsey Williams, Times & Seasons Music, Inc., BMI, Really Big Bison Productions, SESAC, 2015.

"God's Not Through with Her Yet," Steve Chapman and Tim Morgan, Times & Seasons Music, Inc., BMI, Mathis Mountain Music (LLC), 2015.

"Look Up," Steve Chapman, Lindsey Williams, and Tim Morgan, Times & Seasons Music, Inc., BMI, Really Big Bison Music, SESAC, Mathis Mountain Music (LLC), 2015.

"Rearview Mirror," Steve Chapman, Times & Seasons Music, Inc., BMI, 2015.

"Remember Me," Steve Chapman, Times & Seasons Music, Inc., BMI, 2013.

"Say Jesus," Steve Chapman, Times & Seasons Music, Inc., BMI, 2015.

"Stone's Throw Away," Steve Chapman and Jeff Pearles, Times & Seasons Music, Inc., BMI, Jeffed Music, BMI, 2015.

"Whisper," Steve Chapman, Times & Seasons Music, Inc., BMI, 2015.

About the Author

Steve's love of hunting began in his early teens on an October weekend when a member of his dad's church invited him to tag along on a squirrel hunt. Taking advantage of the annual archery, muzzleloader, and rifle seasons, Steve calculates that since he started hunting he's headed to the woods on more than 2500 mornings and hopes to continue that trend for many more years!

Proudly claiming West Virginia as his home state, Steve grew up the son of a preacher. He met his wife, Annie, in junior high school in 1963. In March 1975, they married and settled in Nashville, Tennessee. There they raised their son and daughter, Nathan and Heidi. Nathan and his wife, Stephanie, and Heidi and her husband, Emmitt, each have three children. As Steve puts it, "Annie and I are blessed with four doe and two bucks in the 'grand herd.'"

Steve is president of S&A Family, Inc., an organization formed to oversee the production of the Chapmans' recorded music. They've maintained "family life" as the theme of their lyrics since they began singing together in 1980. As Dove Award-winning artists, their schedule has sent them to all 50 states and to various locations overseas.

A Look at Life from a Deer Stand

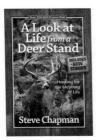

Steve Chapman's popular *A Look at Life from a Deer Stand* (more than 300,000 copies sold) now includes new stories and illustrations as well as a stunning new cover.

From the incredible rush of bagging "the big one" to standing in awe of God's magnificent creation, Steve Chapman captures the spirit of the hunt. In short chapters filled with excitement and humor, he takes you on his successful—and not-so-successful—forays into the heart of deer country. As you experience the joy of scouting a trophy buck, you'll discover how the skills necessary for great hunting can help you draw closer to the Lord.

A Look at Life from a Deer Stand Devotional

Steve Chapman, avid hunter and bestselling author, has a gift for gleaning faith lessons from the glories of creation. This pocket-sized gathering of devotions, handsomely bound in a soft, suede-like cover, invites readers to join in the thrill of the pursuit, the celebration of nature, and the enjoyment of God's presence.

More Great Books by the Chapman Family